MATTHEW RYAN's work includes: *Danny Fisher* (Queensland Theatre 2015 as *Brisbane*), *Kelly* (Queensland Theatre National Australian Tour 2015/ Queensland Theatre 2012), *The Harbinger* co-written with David Morton (Critical Stages National Australian Tour 2014/Dead Puppet Society/ La Boite Theatre Company 2012), *Boy Girl Wall* co-written with Lucas Stibbard (The Escapists/Melbourne Theatre Company 2012/Critical Stages Australian National Tour 2012/La Boite Theatre Company 2011/ Hothouse Theatre 2011/Adelaide Fringe 2010/Metro Arts 2010), *Summer Wonderland* (La Boite Theatre Company 2007) and *Chasing The Whale* (La Boite Theatre Company 2005 as *The Dance of Jeremiah*). Matthew has developed a series of works for young performers through Backbone Youth Arts called *Plays From The Top Of The Stairs*.

Matthew received Queensland Theatre's George Landen Dann Award for *Chasing The Whale* in 2000 (as *The Dance Of Jeremiah*). He received Matilda awards for Best Independent Production for *Boy Girl Wall* in 2011 and Best New Australian Work for *Danny Fisher* in 2016 (as *Brisbane*).

Veronica Neave as Annie Fisher in the 2015 Queensland Theatre Company production at the Playhouse, QPAC, Brisbane. (Photo: Rob Maccoll)

Danny Fisher
Matthew Ryan

CURRENCY PRESS
The performing arts publisher

CURRENCY PLAYS

First published in 2015 as *Brisbane*
by Currency Press Pty Ltd,
PO Box 2287, Strawberry Hills, NSW, 2012, Australia
enquiries@currency.com.au
www.currency.com.au

Published as *Danny Fisher* in 2019.

Copyright: Introduction: *This Happened. This Happened Here.* © Iain Sinclair, 2015; *Brisbane* © Matthew Ryan, 2015; *Danny Fisher* © Matthew Ryan, 2019.

COPYING FOR EDUCATIONAL PURPOSES

The Australian *Copyright Act 1968* (Act) allows a maximum of one chapter or 10% of this book, whichever is the greater, to be copied by any educational institution for its educational purposes provided that that educational institution (or the body that administers it) has given a remuneration notice to Copyright Agency (CA) under the Act.

For details of the CA licence for educational institutions contact CA, Level 15/233 Castlereagh Street, Sydney, NSW, 2000; tel: within Australia 1800 066 844 toll free; outside Australia 61 2 9394 7600; fax: 61 2 9394 7601; email: info@copyright.com.au

COPYING FOR OTHER PURPOSES

Except as permitted under the Act, for example a fair dealing for the purposes of study, research, criticism or review, no part of this book may be reproduced, stored in a retrieval system, or transmitted in any form or by any means without prior written permission. All enquiries should be made to the publisher at the address above.

Any performance or public reading of *Danny Fisher* is forbidden unless a licence has been received from the author or the author's agent. The purchase of this book in no way gives the purchaser the right to perform the play in public, whether by means of a staged production or a reading. All applications for public performance should be addressed to the author c/- Currency Press.

 A catalogue record for this book is available from the National Library of Australia

Typeset by Dean Nottle for Currency Press.
Cover illustration and design by Miranda Costa for Currency Press.

Currency Press acknowledges the Traditional Owners of the Country on which we live and work. We pay our respects to all Aboriginal and Torres Strait Islander Elders, past and present.

Contents

This Happened. This Happened Here.
   Iain Sinclair   *vii*

DANNY FISHER
   Act One   1
   Act Two   44

Dash Kruck as Danny Fisher and Harriet Dyer as Patty in the 2015 Queensland Theatre Company production at the Playhouse, QPAC, Brisbane. (Photo: Rob Maccoll)

THIS HAPPENED. THIS HAPPENED HERE.

In July 1942 the city of Brisbane found itself at the centre of a very big story. General Macarthur set up the war office for the Pacific campaign on the eighth floor of the AMP building on Queen Street and the city rocketed from a small country town on the fringes of a receding empire to the main staging post for war in the Pacific. World War II was quite literally on our doorstep, the threat of Japanese invasion loomed large, our boys were fighting in North Africa, Malaya and New Guinea, and Brisbane was inundated with fresh-faced American troops. There were even disturbing rumours about a government plan to abandon the entire northern portion of the country from Bribie Island up.

This is the world of Matthew Ryan's *Danny Fisher*. The world the play throws you into is painted on an epic canvas—given the context it needs to be—but if you step closer you will see that the brushstrokes are fine, precise and terrifically intimate.

In *Danny Fisher*, you are in the hands of two gifted storytellers: Danny Fisher, our hero and narrator, and Matthew Ryan, our playwright. Both of them are great company. Very often these two writers feel like the same person but if you pay attention there are times when one of these storytellers takes the reins and pulls us into their experience of the world.

Our fourteen-year-old narrator Danny Fisher has his own good reasons for telling us the tales he tells, one of which is that storytelling quite literally gets him into (and out of) tight spots:

STANLEY: Small ones you got to watch. Small ones got a point to prove.

DANNY: That the excuse you give your dick? [*Beat. Aside*] Shit.

They get DANNY *to the ground and punch and kick him.*
DANNY *narrates to escape the pain.*

Danny is not always the most reliable of narrators, especially when it comes to matters of the heart. Unable to accept the truth, he convinces himself that his brother Frank is still alive and with him in the form of a friendly US airman, Andy; he pretends to be Frank to his grief-wracked mother and he almost habitually adds fabulous flourishes to anything that touches his heart:

DANNY: And then she kissed me.

> ROSE *and* DANNY *almost kiss.*

PATTY: That didn't happen.
DANNY: Could have.
PATTY: Not if she fell through the floor and landed on your face.
DANNY: Everything else was true.

And yet somehow, even though we are constantly reminded of our unreliable hero's tendency toward bending the truth, we find ourselves happily running alongside him, becoming more and more involved in his reality as he hurtles dangerously and headlong toward adulthood. We instinctively know that Danny doesn't exactly tell 'lies'; he crafts stories and the best stories are built out of the truth. Danny's stories are richer and have more emotional honesty than a dry retelling of the known history. It is a play after all and Ryan knows the most rewarding and interesting plays do so much more than merely illustrate moments from a recorded past.

Ryan is a skilled dramatist who knows very well that the great strength of storytelling is that it 'reveals meaning without committing the error of defining it'.* *Danny Fisher* deals with a very specific historical context but it is just as much a play about the emergence of an artistic mind. It demonstrates how great upheaval forges our character and that this can be true for an entire city just as much as it can for a young boy on the cusp of adolescence struggling to come to terms with huge forces at work inside him. Ryan has a special knack for pulling us into giant historical events in a very personal, human and idiosyncratic way and on that journey we come to a richer and more complex understanding of the big picture.

I became acutely aware of this sitting in the audience of the QPAC Playhouse for the Queensland Theatre Company (QTC) world

---

* Hannah Arendt, philosopher

premiere in 2015. I had always known that the script had done a great job of building that vital bridge between its own particular experience and the all-important 'universal appeal' that writers of quality always manage, but I could also detect something new in the combined energy of the audience. It was as if Ryan had combined a new sequence of notes to create a previously unknown chord that resonated in a very particular way. I could detect a powerfully close level of identification that the audience had with this particular play in this particular place at this particular time. Ryan's playwriting strummed this new chord many different ways, through changes in rhythm, mood, key, and even right through to bold shifts in theatrical form. Each time it acutely resonated with its hometown audience. Somehow, with the final lines 'This happened, this happened here', the collective feeling of the auditorium was that Ryan had hit on something that was deeply, profoundly 'Brisbane'.

The play shapes and harnesses a kind of unspoken mythic, collective memory of the city and it is something that goes beyond a simple coming-of-age narrative. Sure, Danny is a boy on the cusp of adulthood and Brisbane in 1942 was a country town on the cusp of making a great step up, but Danny is not just any boy and Brisbane is not just any undeveloped regional outpost. It is true that they often function as metaphors for each other but it's not always that simple: the big picture and the small perspective contradict and repel as much as they complement each other.

DANNY: Broken bone.
ANDY: Sorry?
DANNY: The word. Brisbane. It means 'broken bone'. Do you
    like us?

The name Brisbane really does mean broken bone. When I read an early draft I felt the need to look it up just to make sure (Danny isn't always the most reliable of narrators, as I mentioned). The name turns out to be mixture of the old French *'briser'* meaning break and the old English *'ban'*, which then, when used in Scotland becomes a nickname for a kind of fight that is so bruising it results in broken bones. If someone gets involved in one of these *briser ban* fights and actually breaks a bone, the nickname *briserban* tends to stick. There is no indication that the eponymous Thomas Brisbane after whom the city was named inherited any of the brawling inclinations of his ancestors (astronomy was more his speed), but this is still a city marked by fractures of many kinds, including the many broken bones that came out of the open brawling in the streets between Australian and US troops on 26 and 27 November 1942. It's no coincidence that Danny's best friend has a broken leg that didn't heal properly and so on, but I'll leave it to you to enjoy the universe of gently embedded metaphor scattered about the text, alongside a galaxy of classy Easter egg moments (the artful doubling of the actor who plays Danny's lost brother Frank and his new best friend Andy; the absolute fidelity to the sequence and movements of actually starting a P40 Kittyhawk aeroplane and the names chosen for the bullies on Mulvany Street). This is a text that will reward close and repeated scrutiny.

Danny Fisher is replete with richly evocative descriptions of a lost Brisbane as well as beautiful details from Brisbane's social history. This is perhaps best demonstrated in the two scenes where Danny visits the dancing halls. The following is from when he visits the most dearly loved and sorely missed, Cloudland:

> DANNY: [*aside*] Two storeys high and wrapped in windows. Upstairs for watching and downstairs for dancing. A giant light on the ceiling like half the moon carved from the sky. White pillars on every side with angels on top looking down. And beneath your feet, a dance floor that bounces. A dance floor full of Americans and women.

And on the other side of the river, the Trocadero:

> DANNY: [*aside*] Crowds reek of beer and cigarettes. Alleyways stink of piss and perfume. American MPs hunt in packs, bashing whoever they want to. Negroes and music. Soldiers and booze. And then we see it. The Trocadero.
>
> > *Swing music with a heavy beat as dancers swirl.*
> > AMERICANS *and* WOMEN. *Echoes of Cloudland but more sexual, primal.*
>
> [*Aside*] The thumping of drums and the ringing of horns. Men cheering and women laughing. There's a fight at the doors and I push inside, leaving Patty behind. The hall is dark and the

air full of smoke. A thousand people dance to the drumbeat. Americans spin women in every direction. The women curl and twist as the drummer pounds music through their writhing bodies.

Because *Danny Fisher* is a portrait of a city seen through the eyes of a budding young writer, it is also distorted by his perspective, like the city has its own climate controlled by the mood of the storyteller. When he is angry, the city takes on a sinister quality, and when things are going in his favour the sun seems a little brighter.

Of course not all of the personal moments happen on a grand level. A highlight for me was the excruciatingly tender scene where Patty coaches her friend in the fine art of intimacy:

PATTY: Then what?
DANNY: What do you mean?
PATTY: After her boobs come out. Then what do you do?
DANNY: I don't know.
PATTY: Got to do something.
DANNY: What do you do with yours?

She hits him.

PATTY: You perve!
DANNY: What if I do the wrong thing?
PATTY: You touch them.
DANNY: How?

She takes her bra off from under her shirt.

PATTY: Like this.

She strokes a cup. She holds it out to him. He strokes it awkwardly.

It's not a dog. It's a boob.
DANNY: Show me.

She takes his hand, guiding it over the cup.

Like this?
PATTY: That's... what I think would feel nice.

They look at each other. He smiles.

DANNY: Thanks, Patty.

He walks away.

It's an encounter that couldn't feel more like being fourteen and balances the fine art of poignancy and comedy beautifully.

Throughout the play Ryan moves with ease between different theatrical forms. He is clearly a dramatist who has a lot of experience in acting, design and direction. One moment *Danny Fisher* is a serious social realist play, the next an Australian farce, the next an historical documentary, inspired slapstick, a puppet show, a dark cabaret, a Python-esque skit, an epic war saga and then suddenly a genuinely moving and personal coming-of-age drama. And yet the overall effect is one of total consistency. Such are the rewards of setting a play inside the mind of a fourteen-year-old dyed-in-the-wool storyteller—whatever happens in Danny's heart at any given moment in time quite literally happens onstage. There's real respect for collaboration coded into the playscript with wonderful challenges thrown at the company, such as 'Performers create the events of the Movietone newsreel while a Newsreel Commentator narrates the action', right through to a character flying a P40 Kittyhawk fighter plane above a rioting Brisbane. The first time I read the play with a view to directing it I rang QTC to enquire about the budget provision to receive the reply: 'Oh, the usual'. It was a challenge designer Stephen Curtis and I embraced.

Danny Fisher belongs to the citizens of the city of Brisbane. As I sat in the Playhouse at QPAC watching the opening night surrounded by Brisbanites I knew that Ryan had written a remarkable love letter to his hometown, one that spoke in the special language of its people, to their humour and to their understanding of themselves. A letter that revealed the fault lines of their own history and challenged them to take the next necessary steps into a more courageous adulthood.

Iain Sinclair
November 2015

Iain Sinclair is a director, translator and dramaturg. He directed the world premiere of *Danny Fisher*, as *Brisbane,* for Queensland Theatre Company in 2015.

PLAYWRIGHT'S NOTE

My great-uncle Wilfred was coming of age in 1942. Like our hero Danny, Wilfred watched the world of Brisbane transform around him from a small country town into a city on the edge of a war. Wilfred's brother Colin (my grandfather) was serving in New Guinea and would make the strange transition from a soldier to a guard in a POW camp–fighting the enemy one day, keeping them from self-harm the next. And the oldest brother Alfred would become the stuff of legend during the Bombing of Darwin when a Japanese Zero flew straight at him in an open field. It was the one tree in the field that saved Alfred, crouching behind it as the Zero's bullets sprayed past him. The father of these three brothers saw conflict as well, serving in the First World War and losing his arm in the Battle of Pozières.

Those stories have warmed my family's conversations for years. Stories are a bit like ghosts, ephemeral imprints of another time and place. It's impossible to truly capture the past, but we can always conjure its spirit.

There is a Brisbane that was taken from us. Dance halls. Picture palaces. Majestic theatres and grand hotels. All crushed in the well-greased gears of progress. The ghosts of that lost city still haunt us today. Stories and memories on the tips of our tongues, as if all it would take is a shovel to dig through the concrete and discover what this place really is. Like the hero of our story, we reach back for ghosts who slip through our grasp.

This play is my own excavation as well. Those bullies. Those dances. Those heartbreaks. That desperate escape into wild imaginings. We all look back for answers.

We all want back what is lost.

Matthew Ryan

To Jock Blair and Natalie Lindwall. To Louise Gough and Iain Sinclair. To Dash, Harriet, Lucy, Conrad, Veronica, Hayden, Hugh, Matthew, Danny, Guy, David, Stephen, Leah, Dan and Yanni.

Thank you for your love, skill and patience.
And your dedication to the ancient art of making things up.

Danny Fisher was first produced as *Brisbane* by Queensland Theatre Company at the Playhouse, QPAC, Brisbane, on Thursday 16 April 2015, with the following cast:

ENSEMBLE	Matthew Backer
FRANK / ANDY WEST	Conrad Coleby
PATTY	Harriet Dyer
ROSE	Lucy Goleby
DANNY FISHER	Dash Kruck
ENSEMBLE	Daniel Murphy
ANNIE FISHER	Veronica Neave
ENSEMBLE	Hugh Parker
JOHN FISHER	Hayden Spencer

Director, Iain Sinclair
Costume and Set Designer, Stephen Curtis
Lighting Designer, David Walters
Composer/Sound Designer, Guy Webster
Dramaturg, Louise Gough
Choreographer, Leah Shelton
Stage Manager, Dan Sinclair
Assistant Stage Manager, Yanni Dubler

CHARACTERS

DANNY FISHER
PATTY / YOUNG WOMAN
FRANK FISHER / AMERICAN PILOT / ANDY WEST
ROSE / WOMAN
ANNIE FISHER / OLDER WOMAN
JOHN FISHER

Actors playing the above characters should double roles as indicated, whilst the following roles can be played by an ensemble of three actors:

STANLEY
ROBBIE
JUSTIN
JOHN MONASH
ROSE'S FATHER
JOHN CURTIN
WINSTON CHURCHILL
RADIO ANNOUNCER
FRANKLIN ROOSEVELT
DOUGLAS MACARTHUR
NEWSREEL COMMENTATOR
SHOP OWNER
PUBLICAN
RESTAURANT OWNER
AMERICAN SOLDIERS
AUSTRALIAN SOLDIERS

PERFORMANCE NOTES

The play is written for a constant flow in a general expressive space. Theatrical inventiveness is encouraged with a sense of ensemble, play and complicité throughout.

The word 'aside' is used to distinguish when Danny is narrating to the audience instead of talking to other characters.

ACT ONE

DANNY FISHER, *fourteen, enters and speaks to the audience.*

DANNY: [*aside*] The air is thick and wet and the sun burns your skin like it hates your guts. January's got it in for everyone. It has a temper that builds and builds until it's had enough and dumps a mountain of water and electricity on your head. The smell of dirt road mixes with the pong of dead fruit that falls from the trees. Houses sit on stilts, breathing the cool air beneath them. Houses that make up streets. Streets that make up suburbs. Suburbs that make up Brisbane. It's 1942 and I'm fourteen, which means I face two obstacles on a daily basis. One: Entire countries that want to kill me. And two: The Cricket Boys on Mulvany Street.

The CRICKET BOYS *enter with bats and balls*—STANLEY, ROBBIE *and* JUSTIN.

STANLEY: Hey, it's Fisher.

ROBBIE: Where you going, Fisher?

DANNY: [*aside*] These are the Cricket Boys on Mulvany Street. You have to pass them if you want to get to the shops to buy pencils and paper. They're about to beat the shit out of me.

STANLEY: What's this?

STANLEY *snatches a notebook from* DANNY. *They pass it around.*

DANNY: Give it back.

JUSTIN: Another story, Fisher?

STANLEY: Only kids like stories, Fisher.

ROBBIE: [*reading*] 'The air is thick and wet and the sun burns your skin like it hates your guts.'

JUSTIN: He thinks the sun hates him.

DANNY: Give it back!

STANLEY: Or you'll what? Come on. You can do it.

ROBBIE: Bit small for it.

STANLEY: Small ones you got to watch. Small ones got a point to prove.

DANNY: That the excuse you give your dick? [*Beat. Aside*] Shit.

They get DANNY *to the ground and punch and kick him.* DANNY *narrates to escape the pain.*

[*Aside*] They bully me whenever they can. Ever since they saw me jumping around my yard with a towel around my neck like a cape. They'd crossed the threshold into masculinity a few minutes earlier by seeing Susie Whitmore change her blouse behind the clothesline while I, home alone at the time, had decided to give flying a bit of a go.

PATTY, *fourteen, enters and pushes* STANLEY *to the ground. The others step back.*

PATTY: Touch him again, Stanley Bendall, and you'll cop my stiff leg up your bumhole!

DANNY: [*aside*] This is Patty. Patty has one leg shorter than the other which is why she wears a leg brace and finds herself angry a lot of the time.

ROBBIE: Rescued by a girl, Fisher?

JUSTIN: Wait till we tell everyone this.

PATTY: Wait till they hear your nuts can be found in my lunchbox.

They push PATTY *to the ground, tripping her braced leg.* STANLEY *holds her down.*

Get off me.

STANLEY: Get used to being on your back, cripple. All you're going to be good for.

FRANK FISHER, *twenty-two, enters.*

FRANK: And what are you fellas good for?

The CRICKET BOYS *stop, nervous of* FRANK.

DANNY: [*aside*] This is Frank. He's my brother.

FRANK: Takes three of you, does it? What does that make you? Third of a man each?

DANNY: [*aside*] They tremble at the sight of him as they try to do mathematics in their heads.

FRANK: Let's see you do the same to me.

DANNY: [*aside*] Only an idiot thinks he can beat Frank Fisher.

STANLEY: They just fell over. We were helping them up.

ACT ONE

STANLEY tries to help PATTY up. She hits him.

FRANK: I reckon they'll manage.
STANLEY: Sure. No harm being friendly.

The CRICKET BOYS exit, leaving the notebook.

FRANK: You okay?
DANNY: [*of course*] Yeah.
FRANK: Thought so. Mum wants you in.
DANNY: Righto.

FRANK exits. DANNY picks up his notebook.

What'd you do that for?
PATTY: What?
DANNY: Stay out of it, would you?
PATTY: Why?
DANNY: Girls make things worse.
PATTY: What am I supposed to do?
DANNY: Watch from a distance.
PATTY: While they punch you?
DANNY: Yes.
PATTY: Why didn't you punch them?
DANNY: They'd punch me back.
PATTY: They punched you anyway.
DANNY: Thought of a new story.
PATTY: While they were punching you?
DANNY: Yes. About a pilot taking on three enemy planes at once. And he'd rather blow up in the sky than crash. So he flies straight at them again and again. And they think he's nuts and fly away. Good, hey?
PATTY: Should write about a Jap. They're better.
DANNY: Better?
PATTY: They kill more men than we do.
DANNY: You shouldn't say that.
PATTY: Why not?
DANNY: The Japs are trying to invade us.
PATTY: Good. I hope they win. And they bayonet Stanley Bendall and Robbie Macklin in the nuts. Then I'll be a geisha and keep their nuts in a bottle beside my bed.
DANNY: What's a geisha?

PATTY: Jap prostitute. Except you don't have sex. You just make men want it and don't have to do anything.
DANNY: That's not going to happen.
PATTY: Bet it does.
DANNY: Women are going to be their slaves and have their babies. That's what invasions are for.
PATTY: Where'd you hear that?
DANNY: They eat raw animals.
PATTY: What?
DANNY: Birds and fish. They just pick them up and eat them.
PATTY: Says who?
DANNY: Frank told me.
PATTY: We could eat Mrs Thompson's cat to get used to it.
DANNY: I'm not eating a cat.
PATTY: We'll tape its mouth shut so it doesn't make noise.
DANNY: No.
PATTY: That old cow said I was deformed and in the old days I'd've been thrown off a cliff to improve society.
DANNY: Why'd she say that?
PATTY: I was throwing rocks at her house.
DANNY: Why?
PATTY: Because she was going to be rude to me. Which she then was.
DANNY: I'm not eating her cat.
PATTY: I know someone who won't be prepared for the new order of things.
DANNY: There isn't going to be a new order of things. They're not even going to get here.
PATTY: Where were they last week?
DANNY: Borneo.
PATTY: Where are they this week?
DANNY: Solomon Islands.
PATTY: [*calling out*] Here, puss, puss, puss!
DANNY: We're going to hold them back. Frank's going to fight. He'll kill hundreds of them. Fly out of the clouds in his Kittyhawk and open fire and spill Jap guts all over the Pacific.
PATTY: Not if they kill him first.
DANNY: Take it back.

ACT ONE

PATTY: Make me.

> DANNY *tries to force her to the ground. She gets him on the ground instead.*

DANNY: Get off.

PATTY: Lucky they're not sending you. Might need to punch someone.

> *She walks away.*

> [*Calling out*] Japs forever! Long live the Emperor!

> PATTY *exits.*

> DANNY *stays on the ground.*

DANNY: [*aside*] It's easier to write when you're picked on. You just make someone up and make them do stuff you can't. I've written hundreds of stories. My shelves are full of them. I'm great at it, Frank reckons. Hardest part's stopping. 'Cause then you're outside your head again. And people don't do what you want them to.

> ANNIE, *early forties, enters with* ROSE, *eighteen.*

ANNIE: I punched a woman square in the face once.

ROSE: What?

> *The kitchen in Danny's house.*

> ANNIE *mends Frank's RAAF Flight Lieutenant jacket while* ROSE *helps prepare dinner.*

> DANNY *watches/listens from a distance.*

ANNIE: You will too. They knock on your door. Churches. Charities. She called out 'Lord's business', I heard 'War Office', and when I saw it wasn't the man with the letter of doom, I slugged her.

ROSE: I'm not going to be able to do this.

ANNIE: I was your age at the time.

ROSE: Frank's not even scared.

ANNIE: You can thank his father for that. Filling his head with war stories.

ROSE: They didn't scare him off?

ANNIE: Not the way his father tells them.

ROSE: How's that?

ANNIE: Rosily.

ROSE: There are girls getting jobs in the city.

ANNIE: What sort?
ROSE: Of jobs?
ANNIE: Girls.
ROSE: All sorts.
ANNIE: Men's jobs.
ROSE: Take my mind off it at least.
ANNIE: Off what?
ROSE: Frank.
ANNIE: Why would you want that?
ROSE: Can't sit around waiting for him.

    ANNIE *frowns. An awkward beat.*

[*Recovering*] Backyard dinner's a nice idea.
ANNIE: Fitting farewell. How we got started. Backsides in the mud, eating from tin bowls.
ROSE: Sounds fun.
ANNIE: It wasn't.
DANNY: [*aside*] They lived in a tent. And Dad brought home wood every payday. For over twenty years, his hammer echoes down the street as he grows his house. Floors, ceilings and walls. Always changing it, fixing it, but never finishing. Drives Mum crazy. It's unpainted too. The whole thing. Because you only paint it when you're done, which Mum reckons will never happen.

    FRANK *and* JOHN, *forties, enter.*

JOHN: Tread carefully, Frank. Upon entering the female domain one risks not only one's physical safety but also…

    JOHN *tries to take some food to eat.* ANNIE *slaps his hand.*

… one's dignity.
ANNIE: What news from the radio waves?
FRANK: Seems to be a war on.
ANNIE: Nonsense. Someone would've said something.
JOHN: Is he here?
ANNIE: Haven't seen him.
FRANK: Dad reckons it'll be over in a month.
ROSE: Why's that?

JOHN: Bombing the Yanks was the biggest mistake the Japs could've made. Ever meet a Yank, Rose?

ROSE: Not yet.

JOHN: Crazy bastards. Each and every one of them is of the opinion that they and they alone are destined for greatness. A destiny that God himself has given them. Give a person like that a gun and a lot of nearby people are going to become rapidly unimportant.

ROSE: So, you've met one?

JOHN: Several.

FRANK: Dad served under General Monash.

ROSE: Who?

JOHN: He won the First World War.

ANNIE: He's from Melbourne.

JOHN: And he would've won sooner if the Yanks'd followed his orders.

ROSE: I thought England won the war.

> FRANK *and* ANNIE *stop, concerned for her.*
>
> JOHN *takes* ROSE *to a portrait of General John Monash as* JOHN MONASH *enters, posing in portraiture. Only* DANNY *sees him as real.*

JOHN: July, 1916. That's when the war was won. The day they promoted John Monash to major general. The greatest tactician in the history of warfare.

DANNY: [*aside; simultaneously*] 'The greatest tactician in the history of warfare.' Born in Jerilderie, where Ned Kelly once asked him to hold his horse while he robbed a bank.

MONASH: 'Be a good boy,' he told me. 'And study hard.' Nice man. They hanged him.

DANNY: [*aside*] War breaks out.

MONASH: Right, lads. Let's eat some victory.

DANNY: [*aside*] His failure at Gallipoli.

MONASH: Bugger.

JOHN: [*to* ROSE] His victory at Messines.

MONASH: That's more like it.

DANNY: [*aside*] Amiens, the Hindenburg Line and Saint-Quentin mountain.

MONASH: Shit, this is going terrific.

JOHN: [*to* ROSE] Inventor of the blitzkrieg.
MONASH: I don't like to boast.
DANNY: [*aside*] Creator of Anzac Day.
MONASH: Damn right.
JOHN: [*to* ROSE] And the first general of the war to value soldiers more than machinery.
MONASH: 'The true role of infantry is not to wither away under merciless machine-gun fire, not to impale itself on hostile bayonets, but to advance under the protection of guns, tanks, mortars and aeroplanes to the appointed goal and there hold the territory gained and gather the fruits of victory.'

> MONASH *returns to portraiture.*

DANNY: [*aside*] We don't have a crucifix on our wall. But we do have a picture of General Monash.
ANNIE: No more war stories.

> MONASH *exits.*

JOHN: Not that the Yanks ever listened to him.
ROSE: [*bemused*] Thanks for telling me all that, Mr Fisher.
JOHN: Trust me, Frank. You want medals, you listen to your superiors.
ANNIE: I said no more.
JOHN: You don't go running off to win the whole thing by yourself and get shot to pieces.
ANNIE: [*changing the topic*] Frank, we're renovating your bedroom.
FRANK: What?
JOHN: Knocking out the wall, extending the floor and putting in a big bay window.
FRANK: Knocking out the wall?
JOHN: Be the best room in the house. View for miles.
ANNIE: [*sarcastic*] We're really glad it's happening.
FRANK: Sounds great, but I'm not sure I'm planning on living here when I get back.
ANNIE: What are your plans?

> FRANK *smiles at* ROSE.

FRANK: The usual, I guess.
ROSE: Or we'll travel.

ANNIE: Travel?
ROSE: See the world.
FRANK: I think I'll have seen enough of the world.
JOHN: Only one thing he'll want when he's back. Family.
FRANK: So no need to go putting holes in the house.
JOHN: Least we can do for a war hero.
FRANK: I haven't fired a shot yet.
ROSE: [*at* FRANK] Sounds great, Mr Fisher.
FRANK: Sounds great, Dad.

> JOHN *smiles, pleased.*

DANNY: [*aside*] There are places you can sit where you can hear the whole house. Every step. Every word. I like listening to their voices. How they fit together. They sound different when I'm not there.

> JOHN *sees* DANNY.

JOHN: You. Here.

> DANNY *goes to* JOHN.

Why was that cripple throwing rocks at Eileen Thompson's house?
DANNY: She's not a cripple.
JOHN: You stay away from her. She's trouble.
DANNY: She's my friend.
JOHN: She doesn't have friends. That's why she clings onto you.
ANNIE: You can have other friends as well.
JOHN: You should be playing cricket with those boys. Instead of making up stories.
FRANK: Those stories are really good.
JOHN: He needs to grow up.
FRANK: They're not hurting anyone.

> JOHN *takes* DANNY's *notebook.*

JOHN: No more stories. No more cripple. That's it.

> JOHN *exits.*

> ROSE *goes to* DANNY *to cheer him up.*

ROSE: Hey. Wait till you have a big sister bossing you around.

> DANNY *doesn't respond. She leaves him alone.*

ROSE *and* FRANK *exit.*

ANNIE: Did you get to the shop?
DANNY: No.
ANNIE: Why not?

No response.

ANNIE *takes out a new notebook and gives it to* DANNY.

Our secret.

She kisses him on the forehead and leaves.

DANNY *sits on the verandah and writes in his new notebook.*

FRANK *enters.*

FRANK: You missed dinner.
DANNY: Wasn't hungry.
FRANK: Rose said goodnight.
DANNY: Night. [*Beat.*] Reckon he'll be worse when you're gone?
FRANK: At least you disappoint him. How many medals do you reckon he's expecting?
DANNY: Ten.
FRANK: I bet he is. I bet it's ten.

They laugh.

DANNY: Where are they sending you?
FRANK: Not supposed to say. [*Beat.*] Darwin.
DANNY: Darwin? There's no Japs in Darwin.
FRANK: Have to go find some then.
DANNY: You're going to stop them, aren't you?
FRANK: Course I am.
DANNY: How?
FRANK: Fly my Kittyhawk at them and shoot.
DANNY: All of them?
FRANK: Every Jap I see. Swiss cheese.
DANNY: Swiss Japs.
FRANK: Dead Japs.
DANNY: What's it like? Up there?
FRANK: Like you can do anything.
DANNY: Reckon I could?
FRANK: What?

ACT ONE

DANNY: Fly.
FRANK: That's what I'm here for.
DANNY: You could teach me. When you're back. Reckon I'd be good at it?

Beat.

FRANK: Come on. Let's hear it.
DANNY: Hear what?
FRANK: If you think I'm off to war without a Danny Fisher story you're very much mistaken. And make it 'To Be Continued' so I have something to look forward to.
DANNY: He said not to.
FRANK: [*in a bad American accent*] Now you listen to me. You got a gift, buckaroo. A real gift.
DANNY: Buckaroo?
FRANK: [*bad American accent*] You get a one-in-a-million shot at life, see? And what you got, it gives you two-in-a-million.
DANNY: Is that what they sound like?
FRANK: But louder. And they say things like 'goddammit' and 'Jesus H Christ'.
DANNY: Why?
FRANK: [*bad American accent*] Because they're all so goddamn loud you won't be goddamn heard unless you goddamn goddamn!

    FRANK *takes the notebook from* DANNY *and reads it.*

'There once was a pilot…'

    DANNY *takes the notebook back.*

Only one thing for it then. You're coming with me.
DANNY: Where?
FRANK: To rescue a princess in terrible danger.
DANNY: What?

    FRANK *leads* DANNY *to the front yard and grabs a shovel.*

FRANK: An evil genius has hypnotised her into thinking he's the man she loves. He's led her away to a land of depravity. We have to win her heart back to break his spell and bring her home again.
DANNY: [*aside*] Frank's not a very good writer.

    FRANK *picks up a piece of paper.*

FRANK: Write your name on this.
DANNY: Why?
FRANK: It's enchanted. Every person who wrote their name on it came back from their journey alive.
DANNY: This is the milkman's list.
FRANK: Write on it.

> DANNY *writes his name on it.*

DANNY: If we get two bottles of milk it's your fault.
FRANK: Ready?
DANNY: [*aside*] We run through backyards like crazy people. We cross garden-hose bridges and fly wheelbarrow planes. We dance with a circle of washing-line nymphs. And win a magic cricket ball from a riddle-asking fruit bat. Everything's something else and none of it's here. There's no war and no Cricket Boys. For one night, it's just us. Us but not us. Here but not here.
FRANK: We're here.
DANNY: That's Rose's house.
FRANK: Ssh!

> ROSE'S FATHER *enters.* FRANK *and* DANNY *hide.*

ROSE'S FATHER: Who's there?
DANNY: [*whispering*] It's her dad.
FRANK: [*whispering*] That's not her dad. It's the foul beast that guards her tower.

> ROSE'S FATHER *barks like a dog and walks off down the street, exiting.*

DANNY: Did he just bark at us?
FRANK: He thinks there's a dog that keeps digging under his fence.
DANNY: Why does he think that?

> FRANK *holds up his shovel.*

FRANK: Woof. It's driving him crazy. He wanders the streets looking for it. Carries soil in his hands, checking dogs to find a match.

> *They climb under the fence and under her house.*

DANNY: Wasn't she just at our place?
FRANK: This is different.

DANNY: Why?
FRANK: Privacy. You keep an eye out. I'll save the princess. If the foul beast comes back, knock on the floor.
DANNY: What if it's not you the princess is in love with?
FRANK: Who else would it be?
DANNY: Me.
FRANK: [*laughing*] You?
DANNY: Maybe.
FRANK: It's not.
DANNY: Okay.

> DANNY *moves away, sitting.*

> FRANK *goes to him.*

FRANK: Promise me something.
DANNY: What?
FRANK: You have to dig holes under her fence while I'm gone.
DANNY: Why?
FRANK: If they stop, her dad'll figure it out. It's your duty. The brother always looks after the girlfriend.

> DANNY *smiles.*

DANNY: Okay.

> FRANK *removes the floorboards and climbs up into the light.*

[*Aside*] There are noises above me and they turn up the music. I try to look but I can't see into the light coming down through the floorboards. So I keep a look out for the foul beast on a pile of Rose's mum's dusty old suitcases.

> DANNY *imagines as performers enact the war with models and shadow play—a childlike view.*

[*Aside*] And then Frank's gone. And the Japs move from island to island, closer and closer. Planes. Ships. Tanks. They drop bombs on villages and blow up forests to make airfields for planes to drop more bombs on more villages. They raid hospitals and stab doctors and the patients they're operating on. They march nurses into the sea and blow their heads off.

> JOHN CURTIN *and* WINSTON CHURCHILL *enter.*

CURTIN: Australian troops are needed back here to defend our country.
DANNY: Prime Minister Curtin argues with Winston Churchill across the world.
CHURCHILL: Australian troops are defending England. The Japanese will never take Singapore. It is a fortress of British superiority.
CURTIN: And how are you going to stop them?
CHURCHILL: Fly our Kittyhawks at them and shoot.

CHURCHILL turns a radio on.

RADIO ANNOUNCER: And in tonight's news, Singapore has fallen to the Japanese.
CHURCHILL: Bugger.
CURTIN: Can we have our troops now please?
CHURCHILL: Your troops are busy. Don't make me pull my rank.
CURTIN: You can pull your rank all you like. I have the Americans now.
CHURCHILL: Americans?
CURTIN: And I've spoken to President Roosevelt and he agrees with me.

A presidential fanfare. FRANKLIN ROOSEVELT *enters, gives* DANNY *a Christmas present, and poses for a handshaking photograph with* JOHN CURTIN.

ROOSEVELT: Okey-dokey.

Another presidential fanfare. ROOSEVELT *exits.*

CHURCHILL: Australians are from bad stock!
CURTIN: We're from British stock, idiot!

CHURCHILL *and* CURTIN *exit.*

DANNY *unwraps the Christmas present—a toy battleship.*

DANNY: [aside] They'd arrived in time for Christmas. Thousands of people ran to the river to watch the giant American ships wind their way to the city. They march through our streets as the largest crowd in Brisbane's history cheers from the footpath, windows and rooftops. American flags everywhere and for one day everyone thinks everything will be fine.
RADIO ANNOUNCER: We're breaking in to bring you this special announcement. At ten o'clock this morning, aircraft of the Imperial Japanese Navy bombed the city of Darwin. There has been substantial

damage to the city, to the harbour and to the RAAF airfields. We do not know at this time how many are dead. We do not know how many are injured. What we do know for certain is that the war which has engulfed the world has now arrived on our shores.

DANNY: [*aside*] A week later there's a knock at the door. And a man with a letter.

> JOHN *and* ANNIE *enter, separate from each other.*

JOHN: Dear…
ANNIE: Mr and Mrs Fisher.
JOHN: It is my sad duty to inform you that your son…
ANNIE: Frank Fisher.
JOHN: … died in combat in…
ANNIE: Darwin.
JOHN: … on the day…
ANNIE: February nineteenth, 1942.
JOHN: Your son fought bravely for his country. And the Australian people shall be forever in his debt. My deepest condolences to you…
ANNIE: Mr and Mrs Fisher.
JOHN: On behalf of a grateful nation. Signature, today's date, RAAF stamp.

> ANNIE *stares out at the view through the missing wall in Frank's room.*
>
> DANNY *approaches.*

DANNY: Mum?

> *She doesn't respond.*

Why are you in Frank's room?
ANNIE: I like this room.
DANNY: There's no wall.
ANNIE: You can see the city. All those houses. Washing lines. Boys clothes hanging. Like ghosts, aren't they? [*Beat.*] It's your father's fault.
DANNY: What is?
ANNIE: The hole in the house.

> *Elsewhere in the house,* JOHN *listens to the radio.*
>
> DANNY *approaches him.*

RADIO ANNOUNCER: Here now, General MacArthur's stirring words to the Australian people whom he has vowed to protect.

GENERAL DOUGLAS MACARTHUR *enters.*

MACARTHUR: 'By profession, I am a soldier. But I am infinitely prouder to be a father. A soldier destroys in order to build. The father builds and never destroys. One has potential for death. The other embodies life. And while the hordes of death are mighty, the battalions of life are mightier still…'

JOHN *switches the radio off.* MACARTHUR *exits.*

DANNY: Dad?

JOHN: What was the plane they had him in? Before the Kittyhawk.

DANNY: Wirraway.

JOHN: He got me in it once. Took me up. When I fought, it was mud and stink and the two feet in front of your face. Up there. The things he could do. [*Beat.*] You thought it too. You all did.

DANNY: What?

JOHN: That nothing could hurt him.

JOHN *and* ANNIE *exit.*

DANNY: [*aside*] There once was a pilot who was the best pilot ever. One day, the enemy appeared and he didn't want to crash so the pilot flew at them again and again, hoping to blow up in the sky. They thought he was crazy and flew away. But the pilot was losing fuel from bullet holes in his tank. He couldn't make it home and he crashed in the ocean. But he didn't die. He swam to a deserted island and was safe there. But he couldn't get word home to his family that he was still alive.

PATTY *enters.*

The school oval.

DANNY *stares at the sky throughout.*

PATTY: Everyone's staring at you.

DANNY: Why?

PATTY: They want to use the oval and they're too afraid to ask you to move. What are you doing?

DANNY: B-24 Liberator. Up there.

PATTY: How can you tell?

He shows her a booklet.

[*Reading*] 'How to Identify American Aircraft'.

DANNY: Teaches you by their shapes.

He shows her another booklet.

This one's better. It's for Jap planes.

PATTY: Where'd you get them?

DANNY: They sent us Frank's stuff.

Beat.

PATTY: You can cry if you want.

Beat.

She opens the How to Identify Japanese Aircraft *booklet toward the back.*

[*Reading*] 'What to do in the event of an air raid. Step one—Get to the shelters as quickly as possible. If you're in a city building, make your way to the basement and stand near a girder. If you're stuck outside, try lying facedown in the gutter. Step two—Dig a trench in your backyard several feet deep. When the sirens begin, put your family inside it. Step three—Pack a hamper for your stay in your trench. Include biscuits, brandy, bandages, a warm pullover. Why not a scarf? Four—Make identification tags for your family to wear around their necks. This will make things easier for your loved ones in case of…'

She stops reading aloud. She closes the booklet.

DANNY: We have a trench.

PATTY: We have refrigerators.

DANNY: What?

PATTY: Dad reckons everyone's trenches will cave in so he brought home three old refrigerators and put them in our yard. When the sirens start we each get in one. He thinks it's genius. Mum reckons it's so he doesn't have to talk to us during an attack.

DANNY *starts laughing.*

What?

DANNY: You have to sit in a fridge.

PATTY: Enjoy being buried alive.

DANNY: [*still laughing*] Don't forget your scarf.
PATTY: It's not plugged in, idiot!

> The CRICKET BOYS *enter, with bats and balls.*

STANLEY: Trouble with the missus, Fisher?
PATTY: Go away, Stanley.
JUSTIN: We came to see if he wanted to play, Fisher's recent loss and all.
ROBBIE: He can bat if he knows how.

> ROBBIE *holds out the bat to* DANNY.

DANNY: No thanks.
STANLEY: Don't you know how, Fisher?
PATTY: Leave him alone, shitface.
STANLEY: What's that supposed to mean?
PATTY: It means you have shit instead of a face.
STANLEY: We're being friendly.

> DANNY *throws a weak punch at* STANLEY. *It bounces off him uselessly.*

Did you just punch me?
DANNY: No.
JUSTIN: Looked like a punch.
DANNY: It wasn't.
ROBBIE: Looked like one from over here.
STANLEY: I reckon your folks must be angry.
DANNY: About what?
STANLEY: You being so useless. And your brother's the one that carked it.

> PATTY *knees* STANLEY *in the groin. He drops two red cricket balls and goes to his knees.*

> ROBBIE *and* JUSTIN *grab* PATTY *and get her hands behind her back.*

PATTY: Let go!
ROBBIE: Make you a deal, Fisher. We'll leave you alone if you feel your girlfriend's tits right here in front of the whole school.
PATTY: Kiss your dick goodbye, Robbie Macklin.
ROBBIE: Come on. That's what they're there for.
JUSTIN: Show us you're a man.
ROBBIE: She wants you to. She's not even fighting that much. Are you, cripple?

ACT ONE

DANNY *lets out a yell as he picks up a bat and ball and hits it hard. Everyone looks at the sky.*

DANNY: [*aside*] I hit it as hard as I can. It goes higher and higher and no-one takes their eyes off it 'cause it's the biggest hit that anyone's ever seen. It hangs in the sky and starts to come down again. But it doesn't hit the ground. Because right at that moment the B-24 flies over our heads and the ball hits the wing and flies in the side door and bounces all over the cabin.

An AMERICAN PILOT *enters, flying a large model plane in his hands.*

AMERICAN PILOT: Jesus H Christ! What the goddamn shit was that?!

The AMERICAN PILOT *exits.*

DANNY: [*aside*] And the B-24 lands badly on the runway in the American airfield next to the schoolyard. No-one says a word.

Beat.

STANLEY: That was my ball, dickhead!

DANNY: [*aside*] Except Stanley, who says that.

STANLEY: Get it or you're dead.

DANNY: [*aside*] And that.

DANNY *and* PATTY *hurry away from the* CRICKET BOYS, *who exit.*

DANNY *and* PATTY *cross the American airfield.*

PATTY: Hurry up.

DANNY: They're going to shoot us.

PATTY: They're not going to shoot us.

DANNY: They're Americans. They shoot everyone.

PATTY: You want to go back there without it?

DANNY: We attacked them with a cricket ball.

PATTY: You attacked them.

DANNY: What else was I going to do?

PATTY: We're going to ask for the ball and leave. That's it.

ANDY WEST *enters, an American pilot identical to* FRANK.

ANDY: You kids aren't supposed to be here.

DANNY *stares at* ANDY*'s familiar face.*

DANNY: [*aside*] And then he's standing there. Frank is standing in front of me.
ANDY: You are aware that you're standing on American soil? Technically speaking, you just invaded the United States.
PATTY: You mean climbed through your crappy wire fence?
ANDY: Hey, that's an American crappy fence. And if they find you on this side of it, you'll be in a world of trouble.
PATTY: We hit a cricket ball and it went inside one of your planes while it was flying and we were wondering if we could get it back without being shot please?
ANDY: You're hitting balls at our planes?
PATTY: No. We hit it into the sky where your plane was.
ANDY: Which one?
PATTY: A red one.
ANDY: Which plane?

>   PATTY *nudges* DANNY.

DANNY: The B-24 Liberator.

>   ANDY *picks up a plane and gets the cricket ball out of it. He gives it to* PATTY.

ANDY: There. Please return to your country of origin.

>   ANDY *goes to leave.*

DANNY: You're a pilot?
ANDY: It was nice meeting you kids.
PATTY: We're not kids.
ANDY: And you're not supposed to be here.
PATTY: Japs forever!

>   *Beat.*

DANNY: Her legs are two different lengths.
PATTY: Piss off.
ANDY: Then I suggest you get a head start before they see you.

>   *Performers appear, holding broken model Kittyhawks.*

DANNY: [*aside*] They appear out of thin air. A shimmer of heat fades away and there they are in the distance, lying on the ground in the long grass. Three of them. And none of them whole. Each one shot and broken. [*To* ANDY] They're Kittyhawks.

ANDY: That's right.
DANNY: They're Australian ones.
ANDY: We bought them for parts.
DANNY: Where from?
ANDY: Darwin.

> DANNY *stares at the shot-down Kittyhawks.*

DANNY: We have to go now.
ANDY: Nice to meet you, buckaroos.

> ANDY *exits.*

PATTY: What did he call us?
DANNY: [*aside*] We walk back in silence. And the quiet lets in that thing again which, for a while, wasn't there.

> PATTY *exits.*

> JOHN *confronts* DANNY *in Danny's house.*

JOHN: Did she put you up to it? Your little cripple?
DANNY: No.
JOHN: Why were you on an airfield?
DANNY: They made me.
JOHN: Who made you?
DANNY: The boys who dobbed on us.
JOHN: How would they make you?

> *Beat.*

DANNY: [*lying*] They didn't.
JOHN: So why were you there?
DANNY: To look at the planes. For a story.
JOHN: I said no more stories.
DANNY: They don't hurt anyone.

> JOHN *stares at him.*

JOHN: You stay away from there. It's no place for someone like you.

> JOHN *exits.*

> ANNIE *stares out at the view through Frank's missing wall.*

> DANNY *goes to her.*

DANNY: Mum?

No response.

You washed the wrong clothes. They're Frank's. On the line.
ANNIE: They look nice, don't they? Hanging there. Like the others.
DANNY: Other what?
ANNIE: Washing lines.

ANNIE *leaves.*

MONASH *enters and approaches* DANNY.

MONASH: Battle of Hamel, 1918. Unwinnable they all said. Which it wasn't because I won it. 'How?' you ask. Wasn't guns or tanks. Wasn't greater numbers or higher ground. Do you know what it was? Hot meals. Delivered straight to the men on the front line. Brits thought I was mad. But I looked those idiots in the eye and said, 'Idiots? You listen to me. Nothing calms a struggling soul like a piece of home.' [*Beat.*] I'll be on the wall.

MONASH *exits.*

ANDY *enters, working on the Kittyhawk (model) at the American airfield.*

DANNY *approaches.*

DANNY: Thought you were a pilot.
ANDY: Thought you weren't supposed to be here.
DANNY: Are you going to turn me in?

ANDY *goes back to working on the Kittyhawk.*

So are you?
ANDY: Am I what?
DANNY: A pilot.
ANDY: Am I supposed to be?
DANNY: Why aren't you?
ANDY: I was. Didn't agree with me.
DANNY: Have you shot a Jap?
ANDY: I'm sorry?
DANNY: A Jap. Have you shot one?
ANDY: Any Jap'll do?
DANNY: Yes.
ANDY: No.

ACT ONE 23

DANNY: How come?
ANDY: Why does it matter?
DANNY: Don't you want to save us?
ANDY: You do remember me saying you'll get in trouble if you come here, right?
DANNY: I can help.
ANDY: With what?
DANNY: Whatever you're doing.
ANDY: I'm rebuilding a plane.
DANNY: Two-person job.
ANDY: Except that you're twelve.
DANNY: Fourteen.
ANDY: And not qualified in the slightest.
DANNY: I'm good at it.
ANDY: At what?
DANNY: What you're doing.
ANDY: Is that right?
DANNY: I'm great at it, my dad reckons.
ANDY: He does, huh?
DANNY: Yep.
ANDY: And how many have you fixed?
DANNY: How many?
ANDY: Airplanes.
DANNY: Oh, there's been a lot.

    ANDY *offers* DANNY *the broken Kittyhawk.*

ANDY: Okay. Change the oil. [*Beat.*] Something wrong?
DANNY: No.

    DANNY *works on the Kittyhawk nervously while* ANDY *watches.*

Why are you?
ANDY: Why am I what?
DANNY: Fixing a Kittyhawk.
ANDY: Three of them. Enough parts for one to fly. So what's your name?
DANNY: Danny. Fisher.

    Beat.

ANDY: You don't want to know mine?
DANNY: What's yours?

ANDY: Andy West. [*Beat.*] You don't like it?
DANNY: No, it's good.
ANDY: So where's your little angry friend?
DANNY: She couldn't come. She wanted to though.

    PATTY *enters.*

PATTY: I'd rather suck Hitler's dick.

    PATTY *exits.*

ANDY: What happened to her leg?
DANNY: Didn't grow properly. Whenever Patty hurt herself her mum'd hit her for it. Patty broke her leg one time and pretended nothing was wrong for weeks so she wouldn't get in trouble. Bone didn't heal properly so it didn't grow.

    ANDY *watches* DANNY *struggle with the plane.*

ANDY: Everything okay?
DANNY: Yeah. I'm just used to bigger ones. I'm good at other stuff too. Stories. I've written a couple of hundred of them.
ANDY: Is that right?
DANNY: You like stories?
ANDY: Hey, I'm American. We love stories.
DANNY: Really?
ANDY: Whole country practically is one.
DANNY: Where are you from? In America?
ANDY: Iowa.
DANNY: Was that a word?
ANDY: It's an Indian word.
DANNY: What does it mean?
ANDY: 'Asleep'.
DANNY: You're from a place called Asleep?
ANDY: Well, what does Briz-bane mean?
DANNY: [*correcting him*] Brisbane.
ANDY: Breeze-bin.
DANNY: No.
ANDY: What does it mean?
DANNY: It was a guy.
ANDY: What did he do?

DANNY: Invaded America in the War of 1812.
ANDY: Oh.
DANNY: Broken bone.
ANDY: Sorry?
DANNY: Brisbane. It means 'broken bone'. Do you like us?
ANDY: Who?
DANNY: Australia.
ANDY: Don't know much about you. Only what it said in the manual.
DANNY: Manual?

> MACARTHUR *enters and with an instruction manual while* DANNY *struggles with the plane.*

MACARTHUR: *Instruction Manual for Australia.* War Department, Washington DC, 1942. [*reading*] 'Except for the "Aborigines" who roam the wastelands, Australians are nearly one hundred percent Anglo-Saxon stock who, through courage and ingenuity, built a great nation with their bare hands. Modern cities, booming factories and fine physical specimens of fighting men. Australians are tough, they love sport and, like Americans, they live in the present and the future, and pay little mind to the past. You won't find much you can do that your new Australian friend can't do just as well.'

> MACARTHUR *exits.*

> ANDY *looks at* DANNY*'s handiwork on the plane, frowning.*

ANDY: So how's the oil change coming along?
DANNY: Fine.
ANDY: And you realise you're draining the brake fluid into the petrol tank?

> DANNY *stops and looks at his handiwork.*

DANNY: Shit.
ANDY: Fixed a lot of them, huh?
DANNY: I can learn.
ANDY: I think I can handle it on my own.

> DANNY *gives* ANDY *the Kittyhawk.*

Hey, could be worse. You could be the guy who crashed it.

> ANDY *exits.*

DANNY: [*aside*] It's hard not to see it as a religious experience. The lights draw you into the cold air inside. You buy popcorn under Gothic balconies and knights on quests. The glow of the candelabra and a statue of Pan. And with a ticket in your hand you go up the stairs and into the giant golden room. A temple to worship American heroes. Some call it the Palace of Dreams. We call it The Regent. A chandelier hangs from the ceiling seventy feet above. Two and a half thousand seats. A red curtain, footlights and a Wurlitzer organ. The lights fade like a sunset. An orchestra, live vaudeville. And then the movie screen.

> *Performers create the events of the Movietone newsreel while a* NEWSREEL COMMENTATOR *narrates the action. The effect is vaudevillian and playful.*

From left: Veronica Neave as Annie Fisher, Matthew Backer as Ensemble, Harriet Dyer as Patty, Lucy Goleby as Rose and Hayden Spencer as John Fisher, with Dash Kruck as Danny Fisher (seated above), in the 2015 Queensland Theatre Company production at the Playhouse, QPAC, Brisbane. (Photo: Rob Maccoll)

ACT ONE

NEWSREEL COMMENTATOR: In the Pacific, Australians and Americans unite to hold back the invader. Kittyhawks soar through the clouds, piloted by brave warrior poets. Another bombing in Darwin as Mister Jap pushes his luck. But there'll be no invading here, thanks very much. Thanks to our star-spangled American friends. And our own boys in khaki and light brown. Turmoil in Sydney, as Japanese mini-subs attack the harbour, sinking the *HMAS Kuttabul* with twenty-one souls on board. They try to destroy the Harbour Bridge but she proves too tough for them. No such luck for these homes in the Eastern suburbs, hit by Japanese shells, a safe secure family home no more. Meanwhile, in places that aren't Sydney, General MacArthur gives thumbs-up for his new headquarters in Brisbane.

MACARTHUR gives thumbs-up.

The newsreel performance blurs into reality. DANNY *struggles to get through the crowd.*

A hundred Americans for every street corner. And in every Yankee pocket, there's money to spend.

SHOP OWNER: Price is double. Half that for Yanks.

RESTAURANT OWNER: Eat with a Yank, ladies eat free.

NEWSREEL COMMENTATOR: And don't the local ladies love them.

YOUNG WOMAN: He called me 'Ma'am', like I was important.

WOMAN: He took me dancing and listened to everything I said.

OLDER WOMAN: He didn't drink with the other men all night.

A PUBLICAN *lets the women through, but stops an Australian man.*

PUBLICAN: Americans only.

NEWSREEL COMMENTATOR: Not as much luck for our soldiers, taking their intoxication out on an unsuspecting tram by pushing it over, standing on top and throwing prawns at the passing crowd. That's right. This really happened. Prawns.

The performers and NEWSREEL COMMENTATOR *exit.*

DANNY *walks to the Shrine of Remembrance.*

DANNY: [*aside*] The stairs to the Shrine of Remembrance are divided in two. Nineteen steps first, then eighteen, to remember the last time we did this. Flowers and photos of soldiers surround the eternal flame that burns in the middle. On the wall are names of faraway places. Amiens, the Hindenburg Line, Mont Saint-Quentin.

ROSE *enters, wearing a blue American Red Cross uniform.*

ROSE: Danny?
DANNY: Hi, Rose.
ROSE: What are you doing here?
DANNY: Came to watch the newsreel. Learn about planes.
ROSE: Why?
DANNY: [*lying*] Writing a story. You?
ROSE: Work. Got a job. I stop here on my way home.
DANNY: Why?
ROSE: Look at the flowers. Photos. See if there are any new ones.
DANNY: Are there?
ROSE: Haven't looked yet.
DANNY: Right.
ROSE: Are you here by yourself?
DANNY: Yes.
ROSE: Do your parents know?
DANNY: They won't care.
ROSE: I think they would.
DANNY: I'll miss my train.

DANNY goes to leave.

ROSE: There isn't one. Tram got pushed over onto the train tracks. We're stuck here.
DANNY: Oh.

She looks up at the names on the wall.

ROSE: What do the names mean?
DANNY: Where we fought best. Last time. General Monash. Dad.
ROSE: How are they?
DANNY: Dad sits downstairs. Mum sits in …

Beat.

ROSE: Frank's room?

DANNY looks up at the names.

DANNY: 'Amiens'. That's where we stopped losing. Started pushing them back.

ACT ONE

ROSE *sees a photo in the flowers.*

ROSE: Him.
DANNY: What?
ROSE: He's new.

She looks at the flame.

They say it's eternal. Maybe they turn it off when no-one's looking. Does that count as the same flame? Or does it stay on forever? [*Beat*] You dig holes under my fence. Every Monday. I've seen you doing it.
DANNY: He told me to.
ROSE: You never come in.
DANNY: Where?
ROSE: Up through the floorboards.
DANNY: Didn't know I could.
ROSE: You can. If you want.
DANNY: Why?
ROSE: Talk.
DANNY: About what?
ROSE: Frank.
DANNY: I don't need to.
ROSE: Why not?

DANNY *points to another name.*

DANNY: 'Saint-Quentin mountain'. Where we won the war. They'd been fighting twelve hours straight. Only a few hundred left. And up they went.
ROSE: Your dad tell that story?
DANNY: Not to me.

Beat.

She holds out her arms, showing off her blue uniform.

What do you think? American Red Cross.
DANNY: It's blue.
ROSE: Making money.
DANNY: What for?
ROSE: See the world. Before it's gone. Always wanted to.
DANNY: Since when?

ROSE: Forever. Frank didn't. [*Beat.*] When I was a girl, I used to pretend my bedroom was a ship. And I was out on the ocean at night. And I was going somewhere. London. New York. Somewhere unknown. I'd hug my suitcase and spin around as many times as I could and then look out the window. And in my dizziness, all the houses would rise and fall like they were out at sea. And every house had a woman in it. All going somewhere.
DANNY: What's wrong with here?
ROSE: I'll send you things.
DANNY: What things?
ROSE: Things we don't know exist yet.
DANNY: Why?
ROSE: That's what big sisters do.

The city lights dim.

Brownout curfew. In case they bomb us. Every night now. [*Beat.*] How about you?
DANNY: Me?
ROSE: What do you pretend?

An OLDER WOMAN *enters with a* YOUNG AMERICAN SOLDIER, *both drunk and laughing.*

DANNY *and* ROSE *watch them, unnoticed.*

OLDER WOMAN: It's dark.
YOUNG AMERICAN SOLDIER: So they can't see us.

The YOUNG AMERICAN SOLDIER *kisses the* OLDER WOMAN *deeply, squeezing her backside right near* DANNY.

DANNY *watches, embarrassed and intrigued.*

OLDER WOMAN: What if we're beset upon?

The YOUNG AMERICAN SOLDIER *takes out a switchblade knife.*

YOUNG AMERICAN SOLDIER: I'll unsheathe my mighty sword.
OLDER WOMAN: I'm unfamiliar with such a thing.
YOUNG AMERICAN SOLDIER: Hold it tight. Squeeze the trigger. Out comes the blade.
OLDER WOMAN: Show it to me.

The YOUNG AMERICAN SOLDIER *points the switchblade at her.*

ACT ONE 31

YOUNG AMERICAN SOLDIER: Ready? Three. Two. One.

He presses the switch. The blade flicks out.

A shotgun blast. The YOUNG AMERICAN SOLDIER *falls down dead.*

The OLDER WOMAN *screams.* ROSE *grabs* DANNY.

DANNY: [*aside*] We run through the city. Through crowds and laughing and drinking and yelling. And I don't know where she's taking me and we turn a corner and we're through some doors and inside a building and down a hallway and into a small room with buckets and a sink.

ROSE *holds a bucket under* DANNY*'s face and he vomits.*

[*Aside*] I'm not sure how she knew that would happen. [*To* ROSE] Where are we?

ROSE: Where I work. Stay still.

DANNY: Why?

ROSE: There's blood all over you.

DANNY: He's dead, isn't he? That man.

ROSE: Yes.

DANNY: Why?

ROSE: American Military Police. Not trained. Just bullies with sticks and guns.

ROSE *cleans* DANNY *with a cloth and bucket.*

Few months ago we were nothing. Just a stupid little city. Now look at us. Blood on the street. Air raid shelters. Won't even recognise ourselves soon.

DANNY: Is that what they look like?

ROSE: Who?

DANNY: Dead people. Just staring.

ROSE: Yes.

DANNY: Is that what…?

Beat.

ROSE: It's late.

DANNY: I want to go home.

ROSE: I told you. We can't.

DANNY: [*aside*] The room is cold so we lie together to stay warm, her hair in my face and her back against me. I can't stop seeing the dead man in my head and wondering where he is now. To stop thinking about him, I think about her. The smell of her hair. Her American Red Cross uniform pressed against me. I imagine kissing her cheek and her saying she likes it. And turning over and showing me how to kiss on the lips. And her smile as she does it, in the light coming up through the floorboards.

ROSE *exits.*

ANNIE *stares out at the view through Frank's missing wall.*

ANNIE: How is she?

DANNY: Who?

ANNIE: He'd come home smelling like that. Her perfume on his clothes.

DANNY: I went to the city. There were no trains. There was a man.

ANNIE: I'd be cooking and Frank would come up behind me and wrap his arms around me. And we'd dance in the kitchen together. That smell.

DANNY: Something happened.

ANNIE: Hungry, Frank?

Beat.

DANNY *wraps his arms around her from behind. She closes her eyes.*

Stronger.

He tries.

Stronger.

DANNY: I can't.

She takes DANNY's *arms away.*

ANNIE: You shouldn't go to the city by yourself. It's not safe for someone like you.

ANNIE *exits.*

DANNY *approaches* ANDY, *who works on the Kittyhawk.*

DANNY: Why did you stop?

ANDY: Hello again.

DANNY: Being a pilot.

ANDY: I crashed. Came out of nowhere, down I went. Didn't fire a shot.

ACT ONE

DANNY: Now you're scared?
ANDY: Not exactly.
DANNY: Why then?
ANDY: Six seconds.
DANNY: What?

>ANDY *shows* DANNY *the broken altimeter.*

ANDY: Altimeter and airspeed indicator locked up. That's how high he was and how fast he was going when he was hit. Six seconds to watch the ground coming at him. Count it.
DANNY: Six, five, four—
ANDY: Slower.
DANNY: Six. Five. Four. Three. Two. One.
ANDY: You'll excuse me if I don't want to put someone else through that.

>ANDY *goes back to working on the Kittyhawk.*

DANNY: I saw a man get killed in the city. They shot him.
ANDY: You okay?
DANNY: Wasn't like I thought it would be. He just stopped. Is that what people do? Just stop?

>*Beat.*

ANDY: You know, if she is going to fly, she'll need to start first. Problem is, I need to keep my eye on the engine. Which means someone else has to start her for me.
DANNY: I can do that.
ANDY: You'll do what I tell you?
DANNY: Yes.
ANDY: Won't push buttons to see what they do?
DANNY: No.
ANDY: No pulling triggers?
DANNY: No.
ANDY: Hop in.

>DANNY *gets in the Kittyhawk.*

I pretend, you do it for real. Ready?
DANNY: Ready.

>DANNY *moves the instruments in the cockpit.*

ANDY: Coolant shutter to full 'Open'.
DANNY: Coolant shutter to full 'Open'.
ANDY: Throttle to one inch open.
DANNY: Throttle to one inch open.
ANDY: Mixture control to 'Idle Cut-Off'. Propeller control full forward. Switches to 'On' and 'Auto'. Carburettor, full 'Cold'. Fuel on 'Fuselage'. Call, 'Clear'.
DANNY: Clear.
ANDY: Louder.
DANNY: Clear!
ANDY: Ignition switch to 'Both'. Flick switches on 'Battery', 'Generator', 'Fuel Pump' and the three right circuit-breakers. Stoke the engine three times. Now engage the starter.

> DANNY *engages the starter. The Kittyhawk doesn't start.*

DANNY: Did I break it?
ANDY: Just needs some adjustments.

> ANDY *makes adjustments to the engine.*

DANNY: What's it like? Up there?
ANDY: Not bad until you fall out of it. Over the ocean's best.
DANNY: Why?
ANDY: Because nobody owns it. Can't fight over it. Can't invade it. Land of Clouds. Okay. Let's go through it all again.
DANNY: I remember it.
ANDY: You do?

> DANNY *moves the instruments in the cockpit.*

DANNY: Coolant shutter open. Throttle open. Mixture control. Propeller control. 'On' and 'Auto' switches. Carburettor. Fuel on fuselage. Clear!
ANDY: Clear!
DANNY: Ignition to 'Both'. Battery, generator, fuel pump, three right circuit-breakers, stoke the engine. Engage the starter.

> DANNY *engages the starter. The engine sputters and roars to life.*
>
> ANDY *laughs.*

ANDY: Jesus H Christ, Danny Boy. You just started a goddamn airplane!

ACT ONE

DANNY: Goddamn!
ANDY: Goddamn!

  ANDY *exits as* PATTY *enters.*

PATTY: It's weird.

  DANNY *dresses excitedly, getting ready to go out.*

DANNY: What is?
PATTY: All of it.
DANNY: Why?
PATTY: What did she say?
DANNY: I told you.
PATTY: Word for word. As it happened.
DANNY: I was digging under her fence.
PATTY: And?
DANNY: And she stuck her head through the floor.

  ROSE *enters.*

ROSE: There's a dance coming up.
PATTY: A dance?
ROSE: We're throwing it for the troops.
PATTY: And?
ROSE: Do you want to come?
PATTY: You?
ROSE: Yes, you.
PATTY: Why?
ROSE: Help.
PATTY: With?
ROSE: Keeping drunken soldiers' hands off me.
PATTY: How are you supposed to do that?
DANNY: She didn't say.
PATTY: Then what?
DANNY: I said yes.
ROSE: Good.
DANNY: And then she kissed me.

  ROSE *and* DANNY *almost kiss.*

PATTY: That didn't happen.
DANNY: Could have.

ROSE *exits.*

PATTY: Not if she fell through the floor and landed on your face.
DANNY: Everything else was true.
PATTY: Why you?
DANNY: Maybe I make her happy.
PATTY: Must be depressed as shit.
DANNY: What's wrong with it?
PATTY: She's Frank's girl.
DANNY: So?
PATTY: So you fancy her and it's wrong.
DANNY: Frank said to look after her. Brother's duty.
PATTY: Do you know how to dance?
DANNY: No.
PATTY: They dance at dances.
DANNY: I'll copy other people.
PATTY: They kiss too. Do you know how to do that?
DANNY: No.
PATTY: Women laugh if a guy can't kiss. Susie Whitmore pissed herself for a week.
DANNY: I'll kiss like in the movies.
PATTY: That's different. Those women are paid to like it. At some of these dances, they even undo women's bras. You know how to do that?
DANNY: No.
PATTY: Better be careful. They can smell an imposter a mile off. Those who don't belong, don't survive.

DANNY *gets an idea.*

DANNY: You're a girl.
PATTY: What?
DANNY: Show me how.
PATTY: Piss off.
DANNY: I already said yes. If I don't turn up, she'll never talk to me again.
PATTY: So?
DANNY: So I'm supposed to. For Frank.

Beat.

PATTY *turns around.*

What are you doing?

PATTY: Undo it.
DANNY: What?
PATTY: My bra.
DANNY: You're wearing one?
PATTY: I have boobs, you know.
DANNY: What do I do?
PATTY: Grab both sides and squeeze them together.

> *He tries.*

Ow!

> *She hits him.*

DANNY: Sorry.
PATTY: They're not pliers. They're ladies' undergarments.

> *He tugs at it, pulling on* PATTY.

Oh, Danny. You're so manly and efficient.
DANNY: I can't do it.
PATTY: Yes, you can.
DANNY: She'll laugh at me or be taken to hospital.
PATTY: Give me your hand.

> *She takes his hand and puts it under her shirt in the back, undoing the bra.*

There.
DANNY: I did it.
PATTY: Then what?
DANNY: What do you mean?
PATTY: After her boobs come out. Then what do you do?
DANNY: I don't know.
PATTY: Got to do something.
DANNY: What do you do with yours?

> *She hits him.*

PATTY: You perve!
DANNY: What if I do the wrong thing?
PATTY: You touch them.
DANNY: How?

> *She takes her bra off from under her shirt.*

PATTY: Like this.

She strokes a cup. She holds it out to him. He strokes it awkwardly.

It's not a dog. It's a boob.

DANNY: Show me.

She takes his hand, guiding it over the cup.

Like this?

PATTY: That's… what I think would feel nice.

They look at each other. He smiles.

DANNY: Thanks, Patty.

He walks away.

PATTY: No worries.

She exits.

DANNY: [*aside*] The funicular tram is open to the air and you can see for miles as it climbs the hill. Houses and streets get smaller below. You hear it first. Music and laughing and feet on the dance floor. And you reach the top and there it is. A huge white arch, sixty feet high and bursting with light. And you go up the stairs and into a dream world. It's the strangest and most beautiful thing we have. We call it Cloudland.

Music swells. AMERICAN SOLDIERS *dance with* WOMEN *as* DANNY *looks at the ballroom.*

[*Aside*] Two storeys high and wrapped in windows. Upstairs for watching and downstairs for dancing. A giant light on the ceiling like half the moon carved from the sky. White pillars on every side with angels on top looking down. And beneath your feet, a dance floor that bounces. A dance floor full of Americans and women.

OLDER WOMAN: Their uniforms and aftershave. Their 'Yes ma'ams' and 'Hey babes'. Men who dance. Men who listen. Young, handsome, chivalrous men.

MACARTHUR *approaches with his instruction manual.*

MACARTHUR: [*reading*] 'Australian girls are often amazed at the politeness of American soldiers. Australian men are often confused by it. To the Australian male, all those "pleases" and "thankyous" are for sissies. Aussie men prefer the company of other men and a man that likes female company is called a "poofter" which is a man who likes the company of other men. Australian slang is confusing and a whole chapter is devoted to it at the end of this manual.'

MACARTHUR exits.

ROSE approaches, wearing her Red Cross uniform.

ROSE: Danny.
DANNY: Hi.
ROSE: You made it.
DANNY: Yep.
ROSE: You're so dressed-up.
DANNY: Thanks. So are you. I mean you look nice. Tonight.

He gives her a flower.

This is a flower.
ROSE: For me?
DANNY: They were growing outside near the toilets.
ROSE: Thank you. So are you ready to start?
DANNY: Start what?

ROSE gives him a head of lettuce.

ROSE: Take this to the kitchen and start chopping it up. When you're done, start on the cucumbers, then the celery. I'll check in with you by then. You're a lifesaver.

ROSE leaves DANNY holding the lettuce.

PATTY approaches, dressed-up.

DANNY: What are you doing here?
PATTY: Why are you holding a lettuce?
DANNY: It doesn't matter.
PATTY: No-one else is holding a lettuce.
DANNY: I know.
PATTY: You look really stupid.
DANNY: She asked me to cut it up.
PATTY: What?
DANNY: I'm supposed to cut it up. In the kitchen.

PATTY starts laughing.

PATTY: You're here to work!
DANNY: Shut up.
PATTY: 'Ooh, Danny. Peel my lettuce for me. Squeeze my tomatoes. Squeeze them hard!'
DANNY: Please leave me alone.
PATTY: Maybe she'll let you play with her boobs as a thankyou.
DANNY: You're disgusting. You're always disgusting!
PATTY: And you're an idiot. As if she'd be interested in you.
DANNY: Where are you going?
PATTY: To let some Americans fall in love with me.
DANNY: You can't dance.
PATTY: Why not?
DANNY: 'Cause you're…

He stops himself.

PATTY: 'Cause I'm what?
DANNY: You'll fall over.
PATTY: Well, I'd rather fall over than make everyone a salad!

PATTY *storms off.* DANNY *remains with his lettuce.*

ROSE *approaches.*

ROSE: Everything okay?
DANNY: I didn't know I was here for lettuce.
ROSE: What?
DANNY: [*louder*] I didn't know I was here for lettuce!
ROSE: I thought you'd want to get out of the house.
DANNY: I think I should go.

The music changes to a slower number.

ROSE: Come on, Astaire.
DANNY: Where?
ROSE: Where you've been staring since you got here. Let's give it a try.
DANNY: I don't know how.
ROSE: That's what big sisters are for.

They hold each other awkwardly, having to deal with the lettuce.

They dance. DANNY *keeps looking at his feet.*

They will keep moving without you looking at them.

DANNY: I'm not sure they will.

ROSE: You're better than your brother.

DANNY: No, I'm not.

ROSE: I wait for you on Mondays. To dig under my fence. I watch you doing it and I squint my eyes and you look just like him. And I pretend it was all some mistake. And there he is. Right in front of me.

They stare at each other. For a moment, a possibility.

ANDY enters.

ANDY: Hey, buckaroo.

ROSE *stares at* ANDY, *stunned by his familiar face.*

DANNY: What are you doing here?

ANDY: Man of many talents. You should see him start an airplane.

ROSE: You know each other?

ANDY: Andy West from Iowa.

ROSE: Rose. My name.

ANDY: Nice to meet you, Rose. [*Off her look*] How about it, Danny Boy? Mind if I cut in?

DANNY: She was showing me how.

ANDY: Maybe she can teach me too.

ROSE: [*to* DANNY] Why don't you go and finish the salad? I'll be in there soon.

DANNY backs away.

He watches as ROSE *and* ANDY *dance slowly.*

AUSTRALIAN SOLDIERS *approach with drinks, watching* ROSE *and* ANDY. JOHN *seems to be with them.*

DANNY: [*aside*] They stand in packs around the edges of the room. They sweat in thick uniforms. They can't dance in their boots. They drink beer and watch as the women are swept off their feet by Americans. They wait for someone to do something but nobody does. So they stand there. And watch. And wait.

ANDY and ROSE *exit together.*

The AUSTRALIAN SOLDIERS *exit.*

JOHN *remains. He stares out through Frank's missing wall, wearing his old army uniform. He has a trophy and Frank's RAAF jacket. He's drunk.*

>   DANNY *approaches.*

Dad? What are you doing?

JOHN: They said there'd be a storm. Won't come this way. Whole world's burning just over the horizon. Shut your eyes and you can feel the heat of it.

DANNY: What are you wearing?

JOHN: Where have you been?

DANNY: Out.

JOHN: Out where?

DANNY: Just out.

JOHN: You do that now, do you?

DANNY: Where's Mum?

JOHN: Having a lie down. Wore herself out looking for Frank. Wandering the streets. Door to door. No-one had the heart to tell her. Wouldn't listen to me. Kept saying it was my fault. That he wouldn't come home because of me. Because I told him stories and he hates me now. [*Beat.*] I can't seem to put this wall up. Every morning I intend to. Every night it's still not there. A man should keep his walls on his house.

DANNY: What's that?

JOHN: A trophy.

DANNY: For what?

JOHN: Winning.

DANNY: Is it Frank's?

JOHN: Well, it wouldn't be yours, would it?

>   JOHN *goes to leave.*

DANNY: Maybe.

JOHN: For what?

>   *He throws the RAAF jacket at* DANNY.

[*Yelling*] For what?!

>   DANNY *has no answer.*
>
>   JOHN *leaves.*
>
>   DANNY *is alone.*
>
>   *An air raid siren starts in the distance.*

DANNY *looks out through Frank's missing wall.*
Another siren, closer.
DANNY *picks up the RAAF jacket.*
Another siren, closer.
He puts on Frank's jacket, staring at the sky.
Another siren.
More.

END OF ACT ONE

ACT TWO

DANNY *and* PATTY *cross the American airfield.* PATTY *is wearing a dressing-gown over pants.*

PATTY: Slow down.
DANNY: Hurry up.
PATTY: I'm a cripple.
DANNY: Ssh!
PATTY: Why can't we use torches?
DANNY: They'll see us.

> DANNY *looks around, lost.*

PATTY: Do you know where you're going?
DANNY: Give me a minute.
PATTY: You're lost.
DANNY: No, I'm not.
PATTY: Why are you looking around?
DANNY: I haven't been here at night.
PATTY: It's a field.
DANNY: It's big.
PATTY: Why are we here?
DANNY: I need to learn.
PATTY: Learn what?
DANNY: How to fly.
PATTY: What?
DANNY: I need to learn in the Kittyhawk.
PATTY: Why?
DANNY: So when the Japs get here I can fight them.
PATTY: Are you nuts?
DANNY: Ssh!
PATTY: You can't fly a plane.
DANNY: Not yet.
PATTY: Not ever.
DANNY: Says who?

ACT TWO

PATTY: You won't even get off the runway.
DANNY: Bet I do.
PATTY: And I bet you crash and die a horrible burning death.
DANNY: I bet they give me a trophy.
PATTY: For what?
DANNY: Killing hundreds of them. As many as Frank would've.
PATTY: You're not Frank.
DANNY: I could do it.
PATTY: This isn't one of your stupid stories.
DANNY: They're not stupid.
PATTY: Do you know how to take off?
DANNY: No.
PATTY: They take off when they fly. They shoot too. Do you know how to do that?
DANNY: I'll figure it out.
PATTY: I'll turn you in.
DANNY: Why?
PATTY: So you don't kill yourself like an idiot.
DANNY: Turn me in and we're not friends.
PATTY: So?
DANNY: So you don't have any others.

Beat.

PATTY: So why am I here?
DANNY: To keep a look out.
PATTY: That's why you dragged me out here in the middle of the night?
DANNY: There's no point if they catch me.
PATTY: Maybe I won't. Maybe it's against my interests.
DANNY: What interests?
PATTY: Haven't you noticed?

She indicates her dressing-gown.

DANNY: It's a dressing-gown.
PATTY: It's Japanese clothing. This is how I'm dressing from now on. So they know I'm on their side when they get here.
DANNY: They don't wear dressing-gowns.
PATTY: I saw a photo. They're called komos.
DANNY: They are not.

PATTY: They are too. I'm a Jap spy. I'm going to tell them all about your plan. And they're going to kill you the moment you take off.

> DANNY *grabs the dressing-gown.* PATTY *holds his arms.*

Let go.
DANNY: Take it off.
PATTY: No.

> DANNY *pulls it apart. He stops, shocked.*
>
> *She closes her dressing-gown and slaps him across the face.*

DANNY: I thought you were wearing something.
PATTY: You don't wear something under a komo!

> *She moves away from him.*
>
> *Beat.*

Did you see them?
DANNY: It's too dark.
PATTY: Liar. You pissed your pants.
DANNY: No, I didn't.
PATTY: When those air raid sirens went off? I heard some people passed out from fear. That was a false alarm. They'll die from heart attacks when the real thing happens. So will you.
DANNY: No, I won't.
PATTY: My tits just scared you.
DANNY: Maybe I didn't like them. Maybe they're weird.
PATTY: My tits aren't weird.
DANNY: How would you know?
PATTY: A Yank would've liked them. He'd be all over me by now.
DANNY: No, he wouldn't.
PATTY: They've given us nicknames. Older women are 'Lounge Lizzies'. Middle ones are 'Goodtime Girls'. And my age are 'Cuddle Bunnies'.
DANNY: You're not like that.
PATTY: Like what?
DANNY: Those women.
PATTY: What's wrong with those women?
DANNY: Keep your voice down.
PATTY: Or you'll what? Piss yourself again?

ACT TWO

DANNY sees the Kittyhawk.

DANNY: I see it.

He goes to it.

PATTY: You die, I'm putting dog shit on your gravestone. Every day. Different dogshit every day.

DANNY: Just keep watch.

DANNY gets in the Kittyhawk while PATTY looks out at the darkness.

PATTY: Nothing. Nothing. Nothing.

DANNY: I can start it, you know. If I could take off, I'd be up there right now.

PATTY: And what do you do if the Japs show up? Throw your shoe at them?

DANNY picks up the radio and talks into it.

DANNY: This is Flight Lieutenant Danny Fisher. Does anyone read me? Over.

PATTY: You say something?

DANNY: Repeat. This is Danny Fisher, patrolling the skies for enemy invaders. Does anyone read me? Over.

FRANK appears in his RAAF uniform, flying another Kittyhawk.

FRANK: Reading you loud and clear, Danny Fisher.

DANNY: Frank?

FRANK: Affirmative. Any sign of them?

DANNY: Nothing yet.

PATTY: Are you talking to someone?

DANNY: No. Ssh!

FRANK: What was that? Over.

DANNY: Enemy jamming radio. Over.

PATTY: You sound like you're talking to someone.

DANNY: Changing frequency.

FRANK: Changing frequency.

PATTY: You sound like—

They both flick switches. PATTY mouths silently. No response. She gives up.

DANNY: That did the trick.

DANNY *and* FRANK *fly their Kittyhawks.*

FRANK: So what's it like? Up here?
DANNY: Beautiful.
FRANK: How'd you learn?
DANNY: Some guy.
FRANK: Pilot?
DANNY: Used to be.
FRANK: Can't stay long.
DANNY: Why not?
FRANK: Ground's coming.
DANNY: What do you mean?
FRANK: You think to yourself, 'This is it. Your last seconds. These are the last things you're ever going to be thinking.' So you try to come up with something good to finish on.
DANNY: What did you come up with?
FRANK: Us flying together. This is my last thought. Good one, hey?
DANNY: I thought this was mine.
FRANK: Land of Clouds. Not really anyone's.

Beat.

DANNY: Everything's shit, Frank. Mum and Dad are losing it. I can't look after Rose. If I was you, they'd listen to me.
FRANK: Shoot a Jap, you will be.
DANNY: I don't know how.
FRANK: I'll teach you.
DANNY: Really?
FRANK: Few seconds left.
DANNY: What are we going to shoot?
PATTY: At least if there was sun, I could sunbake. Yanks love tanned legs.
DANNY: Enemy sighted.
FRANK: Where?
DANNY: There. In the komo. Enemy tits at twelve o'clock!
FRANK: I see her.
DANNY: What do I do?
FRANK: 'Gun Sight' breaker switch.
DANNY: 'Gun Sight' breaker switch.
FRANK: 'Rheostat' switch.
DANNY: 'Rheostat' switch.

ACT TWO

FRANK & DANNY: [*together*] 'All Gun' switch. 'Armament' switch.
PATTY: Susie Whitmore shaves her legs now.
DANNY: Get her in your sight.
FRANK: Fly smoothly.
PATTY: Said she'd show me how, if I wanted.
DANNY: Trigger on the stick.
FRANK: Squeeze, don't pull.
PATTY: I could get you to help me.
DANNY: She's in my sight.
PATTY: So are there bullets in that thing?

> *Deafening gunshots ring out as one of the Kittyhawk guns fires, the bullets just missing* PATTY.

DANNY & PATTY: [*together*] Holy shit!

> FRANK *exits as* DANNY *and* PATTY *run.*

DANNY: [*aside*] We run through the dark and can't see a thing and there's torches behind us and people yelling and we hit the fence and crawl underneath and we're in the school and then the streets and there's no-one chasing and we stop and breathe and we're out of danger.

> *He smiles at* PATTY, *then realises. She punches him. He goes down.*
> *She kicks him and exits.*

[*Aside*] It's not that I can't see her point of view. I did fire several fifty-calibre bullets past her head at close range. But it occurs to me with some happiness as I lie there waiting for the pain to become more manageable: I can shoot Japs.

> MONASH *enters.*

MONASH: The first man I killed was at Gallipoli. A rapscallion Turk defending his country at the cost of thousands of Australian lives. He looked up to see if we were there and I showed him that we were. But he wasn't. Because I'd shot him.

> MACARTHUR *enters.*

MACARTHUR: The first man I killed was two men. Filipino tough guys who didn't like America buying their country fair and square from the Spanish. Shot 'em both dead with my pistol: bang-bang.
DANNY: What's it like?

MONASH: What's what like?
DANNY: Being a hero?
MACARTHUR: Not too bad as a matter of fact.
MONASH: He was talking to me.
MACARTHUR: Who are you again?
MONASH: General Monash.
MACARTHUR: Never heard of you.
MONASH: I won the First World War.
MACARTHUR: I fought there.
MONASH: And were taken prisoner by your own men who mistook you for the enemy.
MACARTHUR: It was dark.
MONASH: My men broke the Hindenburg Line, overtaking the Americans, who had all fallen over.
MACARTHUR: I was the youngest major general in the United States Army.
MONASH: I was the first commander to be knighted by the King of England on the field of battle in two hundred years.
DANNY: I can shoot Japs.
MACARTHUR: Shot one, have you?
DANNY: No. But I can.
MACARTHUR: Trench madness.
MONASH: Sad to look at.
DANNY: Trench what?
MONASH: 'Soldiers on the edge of battle may let their fear become irrational.'
MACARTHUR: 'Isolate your soldier away from others to prevent their madness spreading.'
DANNY: I'm not mad. I'm going to fight and be a hero.
MONASH: And you think that's enough, do you?
MACARTHUR: He does. He thinks that's enough.
MONASH: It takes more than fighting to be a war hero.
MACARTHUR: [*re:* MONASH] And he should know. He isn't one.
MONASH: It takes the courage of a lion.
MACARTHUR: A will of steel.
MONASH: A mind of Machiavelli.
MACARTHUR: And a dick the size of Florida.

ACT TWO

DANNY: What?
MONASH: Women.
MACARTHUR: All war heroes are fantastic in bed.
DANNY: Really?
MONASH: Julius Caesar had three wives and still had time for Cleopatra.
MACARTHUR: Napoleon and Marie behind Joséphine's back.
MONASH: King Tut and half his family.
MACARTHUR: Genghis Kahn and half the continent.
DANNY: What about you two?

    MONASH *and* MACARTHUR *look at each other competitively.*

MONASH: Wife.
MACARTHUR: Two wives.
MONASH: Had an affair with my wife's best friend.
MACARTHUR: Took a sixteen-year-old Filipino girl as a lover.
MONASH: Had an affair with my best friend's wife.
MACARTHUR: Paraded Filipino girl in front of half of Washington.
MONASH: Was having sex with my mistress when I was called to the Battle of Amiens. Won said battle, returned to said mistress and finished said sex.
MACARTHUR: Was engaged to eight different women simultaneously who all found out from my mother and I lived to tell the tale.
MONASH: [*beaten*] Tit.
MACARTHUR: If you want to be a war hero, you need to bed females. Do you have one in mind?
DANNY: She's seeing someone else.
MACARTHUR: A hero doesn't give a shit!
MONASH: All you need to do is look this filly in the eye and say, 'Filly, you're my filly now'.
MACARTHUR: Don't say that. Don't do anything he says.
MONASH: What's your strategy?
MACARTHUR: Gather intelligence. Find something she likes and ask her a series of questions about it.
MONASH: Rubbish. Seize the high ground. Stand twenty feet away and look impressive.
MACARTHUR: Bullshit. Smell nice and learn how to dance.
MONASH: That's what women do. You're confusing him.

MACARTHUR: The American soldier is an unsurpassed love-maker.
MONASH: The Australian soldier is a bona-fide boner-feeder.
MACARTHUR: The Australian soldier wouldn't know what to do with a woman if one fell in his lap and knocked the beer from his hand.
MONASH: An Australian soldier would not drop his beer!
DANNY: So you think I should talk to her?
MONASH: In the words of Genghis Kahn: 'A man's greatest pleasure is to exterminate his enemies…'
MACARTHUR: 'Claim his belongings…'
MONASH: 'Ride his horses…'
MACARTHUR: 'And have sex with his women.'

> MONASH *and* MACARTHUR *exit.*
>
> ROSE *and* ANDY *enter, walking to Rose's house.*
>
> DANNY *hides, watching from a distance.*

ANDY: I can get you chocolates. As many as you like.
ROSE: Chocolates.
ANDY: Or stockings. Silk ones.
ROSE: Why are the American Armed Forces supplied with silk stockings?
ANDY: Goodwill.
ROSE: So how do you know Danny?
ANDY: We're fixing a plane together. Kittyhawk.
ROSE: Kittyhawk?
ANDY: How about you?
ROSE: He's … [*Beat*] Friend of the family. Well, I'm home now. Thank you for walking me.
ANDY: Rose, it was an absolute pleasure. [*Beat.*] I've said something strange.
ROSE: Just not used to… 'It was a pleasure'.
ANDY: What are you used to?

> *Beat.*

ROSE: Not that.
ANDY: So what do you like? If stockings and chocolates don't impress?
ROSE: Movies. Books.
ANDY: An escapist.
ROSE: Travel.

ANDY: Where have you travelled?
ROSE: See that hill over there.
ANDY: Yes.
ROSE: I've been up there once. You're lucky. Packed a bag, other side of the world. Not the fight-to-the-death part.
ANDY: So why don't you?
ROSE: What?
ANDY: Pack a bag. See the world.
ROSE: You want me to?
ANDY: Why not? America. Spain. No-one's invading there. I hear Germany's lovely.
ROSE: Tell me you don't want me to.
ANDY: What?
ROSE: Say you don't want me to travel.
ANDY: Okay. 'I don't want you to'.

She kisses him on the lips. She goes to head inside.

You like me, right?
ROSE: What?
ANDY: Sometimes you look at me like you don't.
ROSE: I do. Goodnight.

She exits.

ANDY *exits.*

DANNY *emerges, looking at Rose's house.*

ANNIE *enters.*

ANNIE: Frank? Is that you?
DANNY: Mum? What are you doing?
ANNIE: Looking for you. He said I wouldn't find you. But it's you, isn't it, Frank?

Beat.

DANNY: Yes. It's me, Mum.
ANNIE: Where have you been, Frank?
DANNY: Walking Rose home.
ANNIE: All this time?
DANNY: Got talking. She kissed me.
ANNIE: They sent a letter.

DANNY: It was wrong.
ANNIE: Was it?
DANNY: I'm here, aren't I?
ANNIE: Yes.
DANNY: Close your eyes.
ANNIE: Why?
DANNY: We'll dance. Like in the kitchen.

> *She closes her eyes.* DANNY *stands on a box and wraps his arms around her from behind.*
>
> *They sway slowly.*

DANNY: You love me?
ANNIE: Yes.
DANNY: Reckon Rose loves me?
ANNIE: Of course she does.
DANNY: Why?
ANNIE: Look at you.
DANNY: Reckon we'll get married? And have kids and a house?
ANNIE: Yes.
DANNY: Danny must be getting big.
ANNIE: I don't know.
DANNY: Strong as me?
ANNIE: Doesn't matter. You're here. Just you.

> JOHN *enters, unseen. He watches them.*

DANNY: I'm going to fight them, Mum. I'll kill hundreds, don't you think? Like Dad in his stories.

> ANNIE *opens her eyes. She sees* JOHN.
>
> DANNY *sees* JOHN.

ANNIE: I told you. I told you I'd find him.
JOHN: Go home.
ANNIE: Why?
JOHN: We'll be there soon.
ANNIE: [*to* DANNY] You'll come? You'll come, Frank?

> *Beat.*

DANNY: Yes.

ACT TWO

ANNIE *leaves.*

JOHN *stares at* DANNY *standing on the box.*

JOHN *leaves.*

ANDY *enters, working on the Kittyhawk.*

How do you take off?
ANDY: I'm sorry?
DANNY: How do you fly it up there?
ANDY: What do you want to know that for?
DANNY: [*lying*] A story.
ANDY: How do you know Rose?
DANNY: Friend of the family.
ANDY: What do you know about her?
DANNY: Why?
ANDY: One minute she likes me, next she looks at me like…
DANNY: Like what?
ANDY: Like I'm the enemy. Wouldn't know why, by any chance? Could be worth something.
DANNY: Worth what?
ANDY: How to take off.

Beat.

DANNY: You're seeing her again?
ANDY: Tonight.
DANNY: Where are you taking her?
ANDY: Trocadero.
DANNY: That's across the river.
ANDY: Only place you're allowed to jitterbug.
DANNY: I don't know what that means.
ANDY: It's a dance.
DANNY: A dance that's banned?
ANDY: They think it's dangerous.
DANNY: How dangerous?
ANDY: It has moves you do when you fall over.
DANNY: It's not safe across the river.
ANDY: I can look after her. So how about it? Want to help me out?
DANNY: Show me first.

ANDY lets DANNY into the Kittyhawk.

ANDY: Take-off is all about throttle. Not enough and you stall. Too much and you'll scare her off. Pretend she's started. Release the brake pedal.

Three AUSTRALIAN SOLDIERS *enter*—DANNY's *imagination. They speak to him.*

AUSTRALIAN SOLDIER: Yanks throw parties where women wrestle to win sex with them.

ANDY: You listening?

DANNY: Yes.

ANDY: Okay. Now you're rolling.

DANNY: Where?

ANDY: Onto the runway. Line up your direction and commit to your goal.

AUSTRALIAN SOLDIER: A Yank is found in bed with a nine-year-old girl.

DANNY: Commit?

ANDY: Where you're taking her. She wants to know you're confident.

AUSTRALIAN SOLDIER: A Yank is arrested for raping a woman in an air raid shelter.

ANDY: Increase the throttle. Heading to forty-five.

AUSTRALIAN SOLDIER: A Yank stabs a woman near Central Station.

ANDY: She's still with you. She wants it too.

AUSTRALIAN SOLDIER: A Yank walks into the Lyceum Theatre with a gun.

ANDY: Lift her tail. More throttle.

AUSTRALIAN SOLDIER: He chases an usherette he's in love with.

ANDY: She wants to go up.

AUSTRALIAN SOLDIER: She hides in her dressing-room.

ANDY: We're at forty-five.

AUSTRALIAN SOLDIER: She locks the door.

ANDY: Pay attention.

AUSTRALIAN SOLDIER: He shoots through the door.

ANDY: Danny.

AUSTRALIAN SOLDIER: Hitting her twice.

ANDY: Danny.

AUSTRALIAN SOLDIER: And turns the gun on himself.

ANDY claps his hands together. DANNY *snaps out of it.*

The AUSTRALIAN SOLDIERS *exit.*

DANNY: What happened?
ANDY: You crashed and burned. So how about it?
DANNY: How about what?
ANDY: What's holding her back?
DANNY: Maybe she doesn't like Yanks.

> DANNY *walks away.*
>
> ANDY *exits.*
>
> *A refrigerator enters.* DANNY *knocks on it.*

Patty.

> *No response.*

I know you're in the fridge.

> *No response.*

Your mum said you were in there.
PATTY: [*from inside fridge*] Piss off!
DANNY: I'm sorry I nearly shot you.
PATTY: Tried to shoot me.
DANNY: I'm sorry I tried to shoot you.
PATTY: With an aeroplane.
DANNY: I'm sorry I tried to shoot you with an aeroplane.

> PATTY *opens the door. She's sitting with her back against one wall and her feet against the other wall.*

Why are you in there?
PATTY: So my good leg can't grow and my short leg catches up with it.
DANNY: Won't you stay short?
PATTY: Rather be short than a freak. What do you want?
DANNY: He's taking her to the Trocadero.
PATTY: So?
DANNY: It's across the river. It's dangerous. There are fights and prostitutes.
PATTY: I thought you wanted to fight Japs.
DANNY: I do.
PATTY: So which is it? Japs or Yanks?
DANNY: He's going to teach her a forbidden dance. We have to save her.
PATTY: Maybe she wants to be there. Maybe she'll tell you to go away.

DANNY: She won't.
PATTY: How do you know?
DANNY: I'm going to tell her. That I'm going to fight them. Then she'll know I'm not a kid.
PATTY: Why do you need me?
DANNY: I said. It's dangerous.
PATTY: Fine. But I get to be there.
DANNY: When?
PATTY: When you tell her.
DANNY: Why?
PATTY: So I can watch you fail.

> PATTY *exits.*
>
> AUSTRALIAN SOLDIERS *and* AMERICANS *with* WOMEN *enter.*

DANNY: [*aside*] A giant sign on the bridge says 'Plume' and we cross the river to South Brisbane. The air changes with every step. The smell of sweat and fish from the wharves. The lights of the Cremorne Theatre on the right. The noise of the Bohemia Boxing Stadium on the left. And we're there.
AUSTRALIAN SOLDIER: Buy us a beer, Yank! You make twice what we do!
AUSTRALIAN SOLDIER: Take his money!
AUSTRALIAN SOLDIER: He's got enough of it!
AUSTRALIAN SOLDIER: Keep your hands off her!
AUSTRALIAN SOLDIER: Invader!
DANNY: [*aside*] A fight breaks out of the Palace Hotel.

> AUSTRALIAN SOLDIERS *bash and rob an* AMERICAN SOLDIER.

[*Aside*] Crowds reek of beer and cigarettes. Alleyways stink of piss and perfume. American MPs hunt in packs, bashing whoever they want to. Negroes and music. Soldiers and booze. And then we see it. The Trocadero.

> *Swing music with a heavy beat as dancers swirl.* AMERICANS *and* WOMEN. *Echoes of Cloudland but more sexual, primal.*

[*Aside*] The thumping of drums and the ringing of horns. Men cheering and women laughing. There's a fight at the doors and I push inside, leaving Patty behind. The hall is dark and the air full of smoke. A thousand people dance to the drumbeat. Americans spin women in every direction. The women curl and twist as the drummer pounds music through their writhing bodies.

JOHN CURTIN *enters, dictating a letter to* DANNY.

CURTIN: From the desk of the Prime Minister of the Commonwealth of Australia. Dear, Sydney Underworld Gang Leader. As you may be aware, the women of Brisbane are out of control. And the professional prostitute cannot compete with the local amateur. Our venereal disease wards are overrun with young women whom we force to use sewing machines as therapy for their urges. We are losing fighting men to these salacious females, who have no regard for their place in society as mothers and daughters and wives of men. All they want is Yank.

The WOMEN *moan.*

All they think about is Yank.

The WOMEN *moan louder.*

And all that will satiate their urges is Yank.

The WOMEN *moan loudest.*

Therefore, as Prime Minister of Australia, I would like to hire several hundred prostitutes. They will be sent to Brisbane by train to relieve the whorehouses, giving our troops better access to women who have already fallen, rather than felling those we would prefer didn't fall. For the good of the country and for womankind everywhere. Hope this letter finds you well. John Curtin.

JOHN CURTIN *exits.*

ROSE *grabs* DANNY's *arm.*

DANNY: [*aside*] Someone pulls me through the crowd and we're through a door and down a hallway and I see who's holding me.

ROSE *lets go of him.*

ROSE: Danny?
DANNY: Hi, Rose.
ROSE: What are you doing here?
DANNY: What are you doing here?
ROSE: I came here with Andy.

DANNY: Why?
ROSE: To have fun.
DANNY: Like those women?

   Beat.

ROSE: Why are you here?
DANNY: Were you proud of Frank?
ROSE: What?
DANNY: For fighting?
ROSE: Yes.
DANNY: Would you be of proud of me?
ROSE: If it's still going when you're old enough, none of us'll be here.
DANNY: Reckon I'd be good?
ROSE: Maybe.
DANNY: Reckon women would dance with me?
ROSE: If I let them.
DANNY: Why wouldn't you?
ROSE: I'm your big sister, remember?
DANNY: And what's Andy?
ROSE: What's he to you?

   DANNY *kisses her on the lips.*

   She puts a hand on his shoulder and moves him away.

  Danny.
DANNY: Okay.
ROSE: You're sweet.
DANNY: Okay.
ROSE: You can kiss.
DANNY: I practised on a rolled-up shirt.
ROSE: Maybe you should practise with a girl. Like Patty?
DANNY: She's really violent.
ROSE: Someone else. Who's not your sister.
DANNY: You're not.
ROSE: What?
DANNY: You're not my sister.
ROSE: I know.
DANNY: I thought you wanted to leave. See the world.
ROSE: Maybe it can wait.

ACT TWO

DANNY: Do you like him better?
ROSE: Than who?
DANNY: Frank.
ROSE: Danny.
DANNY: The others like Yanks better. They'd rather Australians got killed than Americans.
ROSE: Stop.
DANNY: What would Frank say? If he saw you together?
ROSE: He's not going to do that.
DANNY: If he dug under your fence.
ROSE: He's not going to.
DANNY: If he came up through the floorboards and saw you with him?
ROSE: Please.
DANNY: What would he call you?
ROSE: Don't.
DANNY: A slut!

Beat.

ROSE *walks away, hurt. She exits.*

AUSTRALIAN SOLDIERS *enter—*DANNY*'s imagination.* DANNY *struggles to focus.*

AUSTRALIAN SOLDIER: We beat a Yank in Centenary Park.
DANNY: [*aside*] The Japs bomb Horne Island. The Japs bomb Mossman.
AUSTRALIAN SOLDIER: The Yank pulls a knife and stabs one of us to death.
DANNY: [*aside*] The Jap government prints money to use in Australia.
AUSTRALIAN SOLDIER: An MP shoots one of us in a fish and chip shop.
DANNY: [*aside*] Jap whiskey bottles are found on a beach south of Townsville.
AUSTRALIAN SOLDIER: A Yank stabs everyone he can on Stanley Street.
DANNY: [*aside*] The Japs sink a hospital ship off North Stradbroke Island.
AUSTRALIAN SOLDIER: There's a shootout at the train station.
AUSTRALIAN SOLDIER: One of us is killed.
DANNY: [*aside*] There's a Jap spy plane in the sky over Toowoomba.
AUSTRALIAN SOLDIER: We chase the Yank down the tracks and shoot him dead.
DANNY: [*aside*] Jap subs appear on radar at the mouth of the river.

DANNY *sees* JOHN *dropping pages into a fire in their yard.*

The AUSTRALIAN SOLDIERS *exit.*

DANNY: Dad? What are you doing?

JOHN: There's a man here to see you. He's inside my house. Getting me a drink.

DANNY: Who?

JOHN: They're drawing a line across the country. Goes right through Brisbane. Japs make a landing, we fight for everything below it. Everything that matters. Everything that doesn't, we burn. This is the front line now.

DANNY: What are you burning?

JOHN: Your stories.

DANNY *tries to get to the fire.* JOHN *stops him.*

DANNY: Why?

ANDY *enters.*

ANDY: Hey, buckaroo.

JOHN: It's Andy, right?

ANDY: Yes, sir.

JOHN: That's what he calls you?

ANDY: Yes, sir.

JOHN: Andy and I have been talking to each other. He's been telling me all about the plane you're working on. Isn't that right, Andy?

ANDY: You're right about that, sir.

JOHN: [*to* DANNY] Am I right about that?

DANNY: Yes.

JOHN: Excuse me.

JOHN *exits.*

DANNY *watches him go, nervous.*

DANNY: Why are you here?

ANDY: Rose was upset. Told me she needed some time alone. What'd you say to her?

DANNY: I don't remember.

ANDY: Must've said something.

DANNY: You shouldn't be here.

ACT TWO

ANDY: How do you know each other?
DANNY: I told you.
ANDY: Tell me again.
DANNY: Why?
ANDY: Because that look she gets? Like I'm the last person she wants to see? It's on your face right now. Why is that, Danny?

> JOHN *enters, bringing* ANNIE *with him.*

DANNY: No.

> ANNIE *sees* ANDY. *She rushes to him, wrapping her arms around him.*

ANNIE: Frank! You're home!
ANDY: Ma'am.

> ANDY *tries to pull her arms away. She fights his hands off, holding him forcefully.*

ANNIE: I knew you'd come! He said to stop but I knew you'd make it.
JOHN: [*to* DANNY] Tell her. Say it.
DANNY: He isn't Frank. He's just a man who looks like him.
JOHN: More.
DANNY: Frank isn't here, Mum.
JOHN: More.
DANNY: Frank is dead.

> ANNIE *steps back from* ANDY.

ANNIE: But we danced. Together.
DANNY: That was with me.

> ANNIE *looks at* DANNY. *She slaps* DANNY *across the face.*
>
> *Then again.*
>
> ANNIE *exits.*

ANDY: Excuse me.

> ANDY *exits.*
>
> JOHN *stares at* DANNY.

JOHN: That's what pretending looks like.

> JOHN *exits.*

DANNY *stares at the fire, watching his stories burn.*

MONASH *enters.*

MONASH: Newspapers never believed I was a great man. Said I was pretending. Exaggerating how things were. You should have seen them. Those men who ran up Saint-Quentin mountain. Twelve hours of fighting, only a few hundred left. One command and up they went. 'The guns unrepentin', the charge unrelenting, remember, remember the gods of Saint-Quentin.' But we didn't. All they focused on was Gallipoli. They'd only let us be failures. Normal. They just wouldn't believe that we were incredible.

MONASH *looks at the sky.* DANNY *follows his gaze.*

MONASH *exits.*

DANNY *stares at the sky.* PATTY *approaches, on the school oval.*

PATTY: You left me behind.

No response.

Did you look for me?

DANNY: There's a Jap up there. Keeps circling around. Around and around. No-one's noticed him.

PATTY: It's an American, Danny.

DANNY: When he gets lower, I'll fly up and get him.

PATTY: We're supposed to go to class.

DANNY: You don't think I can. You think I'm an idiot. Like everyone else.

PATTY: I think you should come inside.

DANNY: I reckon it's a Zero. Or a type ninety-seven. Depends how high.

PATTY: Did you talk to her?

DANNY: If it's a ninety-seven you go for the fuel tanks.

PATTY: Did she laugh at you?

DANNY: If it's a Zero you hit it anywhere.

PATTY: I don't care that you're an idiot.

DANNY: You make him bank to the side and cut him in half.

PATTY: I love you.

Beat.

DANNY: You're just a kid. You're too young for me now.

She fights back tears.

ACT TWO

PATTY: They're not going to get here. No matter how much you want them to.

    PATTY *leaves.*

    ANDY *enters. The American airfield.*

ANDY: So I'm Frank? [*Beat*] How did he die?
DANNY: Darwin.
ANDY: A pilot?
DANNY: [*re: Kittyhawk*] Is it finished?
ANDY: Was she in love with him?
DANNY: Will it fly?
ANDY: Why do you want to know that?
DANNY: There's a Jap up there.
ANDY: That's one of ours.
DANNY: What if it isn't?
ANDY: They're not going to get here, Danny.
DANNY: Maybe they will.
ANDY: They won't.
DANNY: They're supposed to.
ANDY: I think you should leave.
DANNY: Why?
ANDY: This is no place for someone like you.
DANNY: Like what?
ANDY: You.
DANNY: I belong here more than you do.
ANDY: This is American soil, Danny. America, whether you like it or not. I'm getting an MP. That man is going to arrest you. So you cross that fence before he gets here.

    ANDY *goes to leave.*

DANNY: You're just scared. You're scared because you crashed. Because you failed.

    DANNY *shoves* ANDY.

DANNY: I'd be better.
ANDY: Danny.

    DANNY *shoves him again.*

DANNY: I'm better than you! I'm better than you, Frank!

DANNY *stops, hearing himself.*

They stare at each other.

ANDY: Goodbye, Danny.

ANDY *leaves.*

DANNY *stands alone.*

DANNY: [*aside*] Everything's quiet. There's no-one to fight.

The AUSTRALIAN SOLDIERS *enter—*DANNY*'s imagination.*

AUSTRALIAN SOLDIER: It starts small.

AUSTRALIAN SOLDIER: Just a thought in your head.

DANNY: [*aside*] I look at the airfield. American soil.

AUSTRALIAN SOLDIER: There's a line you draw.

AUSTRALIAN SOLDIER: Only so much you'll take.

DANNY: [*aside*] American planes. American hangers.

AUSTRALIAN SOLDIER: Another fight.

AUSTRALIAN SOLDIER: One of them has a gun.

AUSTRALIAN SOLDIER: One of us is dead.

DANNY: [*aside*] The invaders aren't coming. They're here already.

AUSTRALIAN SOLDIER: Men hear the shot.

AUSTRALIAN SOLDIER: Soldiers come running.

They put Frank's RAAF jacket on DANNY.

AUSTRALIAN SOLDIER: One hundred becomes two hundred.

DANNY: [*aside*] Two hundred becomes five hundred.

AUSTRALIAN SOLDIER: Five becomes a thousand.

DANNY & AUSTRALIAN SOLDIERS: [*all together*] A thousand becomes two thousand. Two thousand becomes four thousand.

DANNY *climbs into the Kittyhawk.*

DANNY: [*aside*] We fill the city. We hunt Yanks and bash them.

AUSTRALIAN SOLDIER: Coolant shutter, full.

DANNY: [*aside*] We destroy their PX.

AUSTRALIAN SOLDIER: Throttle, open.

DANNY: [*aside*] And the American Red Cross.

AUSTRALIAN SOLDIER: Propeller, full forward.

DANNY: [*aside*] We throw bricks at their heads, smashing their faces.

AUSTRALIAN SOLDIER: Gun switch.

AUSTRALIAN SOLDIER: Armament switch.
DANNY: [*aside*] Screaming at them.
AUSTRALIAN SOLDIERS: [*all together*] Clear!
DANNY: [*aside*] 'You're not better than us!'
AUSTRALIAN SOLDIER: Stoke the engine.
DANNY: Engage the starter.

The Kittyhawk starts.

AUSTRALIAN SOLDIER: It's a riot.
AUSTRALIAN SOLDIER: A battle.
AUSTRALIAN SOLDIER: Brisbane's war.
DANNY: [*aside*] I start to move.
AUSTRALIAN SOLDIER: We surround his building.
DANNY: [*aside*] I'm on the runway.
AUSTRALIAN SOLDIER: Men in their thousands.
DANNY: [*aside*] Andy is chasing me. Yanks run from hangers.
AUSTRALIAN SOLDIER: Passing Yanks over our heads.

From left: Hugh Parker, Matthew Backer and Daniel Murphy as Australian Soldiers, with Dash Kruck as Danny Fisher (foreground), in the 2015 Queensland Theatre Company production at the Playhouse, QPAC, Brisbane. (Photo: Rob Maccoll)

DANNY: [*aside*] Throttle at thirty.
AUSTRALIAN SOLDIER: Dumping them in the middle.
DANNY: [*aside*] Thirty-five. Forty.
AUSTRALIAN SOLDIER: Kicking and bashing them with no way out.
DANNY: [*aside*] Forty. Forty-five.
AUSTRALIAN SOLDIER: It's your turn, MacArthur!
DANNY: [*aside*] It starts to lift.
AUSTRALIAN SOLDIER: Come out and face us!
DANNY: [*aside*] I see the sky.
AUSTRALIAN SOLDIER: Face your enemy!
DANNY: [*aside*] The wheels leave the ground. I'm in the air. The engine stalls. I don't know what to do. The plane tips forward. The ground is coming at me.

> *The Kittyhawk crashes.*
>
> ANDY *carries* DANNY *away from the crash. He puts* DANNY *down.*
>
> DANNY *is half conscious.* ANDY *puts on the RAAF jacket.* FRANK *smiles and exits.*
>
> DANNY *is in hospital, wearing a leg brace.*
>
> JOHN *enters. They stare at each other.*

I'm sorry.

> *Beat.*

JOHN: Your American took the blame. They sent him back where he came from.
DANNY: Iowa.
JOHN: Saved your life. Pulled you from a burning aeroplane. What were you thinking?
DANNY: I don't know.
JOHN: Had to be something.
DANNY: If I was like him, you'd…

> DANNY *can't finish. It hits* JOHN *hard.*
>
> *Beat.*

JOHN: You're not. [*Beat*] You're too much like me.

> DANNY *looks at* JOHN, *surprised.*

ACT TWO

ANNIE *enters—a different moment of time to* JOHN.

She holds DANNY's *hand.*

ANNIE: What was it like? When he crashed.
DANNY: Fast. Loud.
ANNIE: More.
DANNY: Smoke.
ANNIE: More.
DANNY: Smelled like fuel. Everything burning. Then nothing.

Beat.

ANNIE: He's gone.
DANNY: Yes.

She hugs DANNY.

JOHN: Your mother put Frank's wall up. Locked herself in. Wouldn't come out until it was done. [*Beat.*] Looks terrible. We should pretend it doesn't.
DANNY: Okay.

JOHN *holds out a new notebook.* DANNY *takes it.*

JOHN *and* ANNIE *move away.*

They see each other. They hold hands. They leave together.

PATTY *enters.*

PATTY: You've got turds for brains, Danny Fisher. If you fell over and cracked your skull open, people'd go, 'What's that smell?', and it'd be turds.
DANNY: I know.
PATTY: No, you don't. That's the turds talking.
DANNY: I flew, didn't I?
PATTY: For three seconds. Win the war while you were five feet off the ground?
DANNY: Where's your dressing gown?
PATTY: Japs are losing. I'm an American spy now. They're better anyway.
DANNY: Is everyone laughing at me?
PATTY: No. They all think you're a legend.

DANNY: Really?
PATTY: Not for long but. I'm starting a rumour.
DANNY: What rumour?
PATTY: Because of your injuries you experience difficulty not shitting yourself when you laugh.
DANNY: Why are you doing that?
PATTY: So you don't become popular. Have to stay friends with me.

> *Beat.*
>
> *He kisses her on the lips. She stares at him as he does it.*
>
> *The kiss parts.*

You're shit at that.
DANNY: Where are you going?
PATTY: To tell everyone how shit you are.
DANNY: Please don't start that rumour.
PATTY: Learn to kiss then.
DANNY: Slow down so I can.
PATTY: You hurry up.

> PATTY *exits.*

DANNY: [*aside*] My broken leg never heals properly and I limp worse than Patty, which Patty thinks is hilarious. When they let me go home, I stop at Rose's house. Her Dad tells me she's gone. Off to see the world. We never see her again. Sometimes at night, I spin in my room and look out at the houses, rising and falling. And I imagine her in one, crossing the ocean. [*Beat*] The newspapers never mention the riot. They pretend it didn't happen. That everything's normal. So people forget. But everyone wants to hear my story. And I tell it to anyone who asks. And every time I tell it, it gets bigger and better. And if someone laughs at me and says it's not true, I just smile and I tell them, 'This happened. This happened here.'

THE END

www.currency.com.au

Visit our website to:
- Buy your books online
- Browse our full list of titles, from plays to screenplays, books on theatre, film and music, and more
- Choose a play for your school or amateur performance group by cast size and gender
- Obtain information about performance rights
- For students, read our study guides
- For teachers, access syllabus and other relevant information
- Sign up for our email newsletter

The performing arts publisher

www.ingramcontent.com/pod-product-compliance
Lightning Source LLC
Chambersburg PA
CBHW050019090426
42734CB00021B/3343